Me-conomics

Socialized Economic Sustainability

Abstract

Me-conomics is the study of the socialized self, as it exists within an economic system. These root values precede employment and help people make meaning out of their work environment. They also create social adherence out of their work environments based upon the judgment of actions through these theoretical values. As nations socialize their populations through childhood, school and work they further embed these concepts and enhance them. When such socialization of values is weakened or takes on different forms there is the potential for conflict and poor workplace productivity. Organizations and government can enhance the sustainability of their economic and social system by encouraging the productive behaviors of life, liberty, and pursuit of happiness through the scientific constructs of employee satisfaction, freedom of thought and motivation. The work will contain some theoretical and specific models that can be used to encourage organizations to take a vantage point that furthers their financial performances in ways that are ethical. The governmental and business owners hold within their hand a great power if that if tapped will change the lives and course of a nation.

Acknowledgements

This book is first dedicated to my children and family. They are the future and the hope is to make it as bright as possible for them. I would also like to acknowledge my colleagues and administrators as Ashford University who helped me think through and review some of the material. Specific mention of Dr. Andree Swanson who was supportive of my endeavors and reviewed a number of chapters. Furthermore, I would like to dedicate this to the readers who may realize it as something beneficial to their organizational and governmental approaches. Even if they do not find all of the solutions needed in a complex world, it is hoped that this work encourages them to think about how their specific view point impacts a wider group of people. If it offers them, the opportunity to pause for just a moment it has completed its function.

Table of Contents

Introduction 5

Chapter 1: Society 14

Chapter 2: Employee Reality Construction 51

Chapter 3: Socialized Self 83

Chapter 4: Economic Realities 105

Chapter 5: Economic Theories 135

Chapter 6: Me-conomics Formula 166

Chapter 7: Innovation 200

Chapter 8: Employee Satisfaction 218

Chapter 9: Employee Motivation 237

Chapter 10: Final Chapter 268

References 296

Introduction

Me-conomics is the study of how business and psychology impact each other in intricate ways that few people are cognizant of due to its subtle but powerful influences. The main postulates of Me-conomics Theory are that humans are naturally seeking self-preservation, self-preservation is fulfilled through gainful employment, gainful employment is bound to financial networks, and financial networks impact value systems, which in turn can predict behavior based upon adherents logic (reality). The book is focused on showing a methodology on how to transform a company from lackluster performance into a profitable and more ethical entity. What many business theorists and consultants fail to acknowledge is that true organizational change is much deeper than the adjustment of a few policies & procedures and subsequent executive "lip service". True transformation requires the adjustment of the entire organization and the development of new ways of impacting employee thinking for higher levels of self-actualization. It is this failure of executive leaders to create changes using multiple perspectives and long-reaching policies that make many superficial adjustments resisted by organizational members and mute in their financial impact. Making changes in a wide and deep manner can help in fostering innovation, motivation, and creativity by aligning employee's decision-making processes more closely to environmental demands. It is this alignment of environmental demands and internal decision processes that creates the greatest opportunity to develop products and services that have useful utility within the market. Thus me-conomics attempts to improve employee satisfaction and financial profits while creating a more ethical business environment.

The "Me" in Me-conomics is the socialized self as it exists within a natural modeled economic system. Organizations that understand and implement changes within their financial networks can impact the underlining values and root logic that employees use to make decisions within their environments. Doing so, in a positive manner, would create higher levels of firm production and individual choice. Investors would benefit their bottom lines by building the foundations of success that are inherent in each employee's self-interest. The Me-conomic's uses an $OS=(ES+ER+EF)/3$ formula to gauge organization's innovative strength and future viability in fast-paced intellectual markets. Yet the concepts may apply also to nearly any business as it seeks to gain a foothold in the global economy and overcome internal operational challenges.

Let us assume for a moment that employee A hires employee B. Employee B is socialized into the value system of employee A and begins to adapt this value system due to the inherent financial benefits embedded within that system. For example, if you follow the rules of the system, you are encouraged by your boss, solve practical problems, etc... you are more likely to obtain additional compensation, recognition, and social praise. Employee satisfaction, employee rewards, and employee intellectual freedom can create higher levels of innovation and efficiency if in proper balance and reinforcement. It is important to understand that employee A and B live within a financial vine that moves upwards to more influential and financially successful individuals who also define society's values. It is precisely these individuals that create overt and subvert values to protect their financial interests (needs gratification) and project those values onto others.

Imagine a new employee who has entered into their very first job. They are introduced to their manager and other internal stakeholders within the organization. From the day the new employee walks through the creaky door he/she will continually make meaning from the understanding derived from of the expectations of people they meet. Some employee will also ask questions to clear up confusion in areas that are not well defined in their understandings. It is their understanding through the language of others that create vantage points and define employee reality. This process occurs in all organizations in the world and is considered the socialization process that all employees must successfully navigate. Even though the fastest levels of socialization occur in the beginning of the employment process it will continue throughout their time in the organization as the environment, values, methods and employees adjust. Thus the nature and personality of their boss, and other management members, will be internalized as a way of viewing and approaching the working day. Each person enters the workplace with pre-existing patterns and methodologies and then adjusts these patterns over time to be effective in their search for environmental validation.

Human behavior can be measurable on an individual, group or societal level. It is possible to understand the developmental stage of an organization in its ethical level and its pathways to growth according to the three principles of the theory. Each of the three components of the theory is discussed toward the end of the book. In brief, where a financial synapse occurs (financial exchange) people transfer values, expectations and norms. In time, such transference creates employee logic embedded within organizational culture. It is this culture that influences the overall intellectual ability and potential capacity of employees and the earning potential of the organization. Me-conomics provides its own justification throughout this book that will help organizations understand cultural influences and develop more ethically sound organizations where employees are free to act and develop to their highest state possible.

When employees are not free to make meaning and find appropriate cultural framework within their organizations their behaviors will be more focused on survival than actual

improvement. Poorly managed workplaces eventually fail to adjust
to their environment due to employee resistance and
underdevelopment. An organization focused on controlling versus
developing their employees will find that new ideas are not
generated to overcome challenges, labor costs will be high, and
revenues through market share will continually decline. In the end,
such organizations will become ineffective while their more
enlightened competitors will continue to grow in both revenue and
influence.

Dr. Drucker, a well-known management theorist, believed
that ethical value systems have a huge impact on business success
(Nelson, 1977). While many economists were running statistical
analysis on economic drivers Dr. Drucker began to take a new
route focused more on the ethical responsibilities of business. Me-
conomics further helps to explain how values can impact, improve
upon, and create synergy by marrying the concepts of values and
finance into a more cohesive theory of human motivation. It
furthers Dr. Druckers concepts of ethical behavior by
moving closer to the root of self interest and survival that make
ethics practical and productive. The structure, development, and

human rights within organizations can be a benefit for both the organization and the investors who desire higher profit margins from the capitalization of such human improvements.

The theory will also discuss groups within groups and how this impacts the functioning of the general system. Such groups can create higher levels of innovation if harnessed well and encouraged to adopt positive communal or individual values through appropriate reward and recognition mechanisms. It is also possible that such groups can be destructive and self-seeking which thereby create less efficiency and innovation. Efficiency of an economic system can be thought of as alignment of all groups, members, and financial vines to a single (or few) underlying objective (s) that are in coherence with root logic of needs fulfillment. When subtle psychological pressure to perform and develop human capital within an organization exists such companies can reap the financial rewards of such successes through overall organizational development that leads directly to new market approaches.

Me-conomics doesn't attempt to replace existing theories but tries to combine a number of them into a cohesive whole. New theories do not always destroy older theories. It is possible to have a higher order theory that groups together a number of lower level theories (Kuhn, 1996). Some might even argue that integrating theories is where a higher level truth exists. "*Today, interdisciplinary and integrative studies, long on the edges of academic life, are moving toward the center, responding both to new intellectual and to pressing human problems* (Boyer, 1990, pg.21)" Each theory is a piece of an overall puzzle that explains a particular aspect of a phenomenon. When a theory can draw together multiple theories into a more parsimonious whole it has scientific value. A strong theory will have the following three components (Blanchard & Thatcher, 2012):

1. Explains facts as simply as possible,

2. Predicts future events, and

3. Provides information on what can be done to prevent undesirable things from happening.

Me-conomics is the attempt to create ethical business practices that are rooted in the best interests of society, the organization and the individual. It creates a momentum and incentive for engaging in ethical activity. According to the Theory of

Moral Sentiments the selfish motives of men are changed by interaction to yield the most unexpected of results: social harmony. With ethical standards it is possible for men to do what is in their best interest while still developing a stronger society. This is possible only by understanding the inherent needs of man to be productive, work for both collective and individual interest, as well as the desire to find homeostasis in their lives. This requires an analysis of the inner workings of man as a feeling thinking, and social creature. To come to new insight we must question our environment, and that which we currently perceive as reality, in order to form stronger understands and create future realities.

Chapter 1
Society
De Omnibus Dubitandum!
(We must doubt everything!)

We Must Doubt Everything!

A very popular error: having the courage of one's convictions: rather it is a matter of having the courage for an attack on one's convictions!!!-Nietzsche

Society comprises the group of people we live, associate, and make our living with. Our society has a profound impact on how we think and the patterns we use to navigate our lives. The values and premises of society also influence the perspectives and the root belief systems workers carry with them as they enter into gainful employment. Understanding the basic values of American society can help to create and develop higher levels of organizational achievement through the alignment of individual and corporate culture with existing societal perspectives. The closer the alignment of organizational values with societal values the fewer resources needed for socializing others to productive expectations and therefore less wasteful conflicts. These values can determine whether an organization will succeed and develop over time within the greater national context or will suffer the crushing defeat of inefficient viability. To understand the societal context can further help leaders understand the basic assumptions and methods employees use to navigate their work environment. This understanding is framed in further fostering innovation, motivation, and employee satisfaction. Progressive organizational structure should encourage that which is positive about human development while discouraging that which is negative.

To understand societal values it is important to turn to those philosophers and their economic perspectives that changed the way Americans view their world. Adam Smith, the founder of modern economic principles, believed that wealth was a manifestation of society. The book, Wealth of Nations, sparked a completely new way of thinking about global and continental markets. Such beliefs introduced concepts of a *free market* where goods and products moved from one part of the world to another in an attempt to satisfy society's needs. It was through this global commerce that the wealth of nations increased. The more a society can produce and market their products the more wealthy society becomes. Even though it is intuitive to assume that those who purchased products were satisfying some type of need; his book did not explicitly highlight this concept.

The Great Transformation further sheds light on Adam Smith's thinking, "*wealth was to him merely an aspect of the life of the community, to the purposes of which it remained subordinate*"(Polayni, 1968, p. 111). Wealth was seen as a subordinate benefit of living in society. However, this concept makes the fatal mistake of assuming that collective society did not ban together first for resource sharing and survival purposes before considering the other benefits. To look at the historical development of society it is possible to see how farming, animal husbandry, and other innovations in needs obtainment sparked ever larger communities and cities. The more resources available through these inventions the larger and more sophisticated society became due to its ability to handle more complex structures. Society is founded on the concept of mutual self-interest and higher levels of economic gain.

Mark Pagel in his book Wired for Culture discusses how Darwinian concepts help us understand that man is a social creature and his very existence is based upon collective abilities (Pagel, 2012). His premise is that man developed beyond biological disposition and determinants of behavior to more conscious transference of knowledge that can influence behavior within a social context. The human being is prewired for collective action in order to serve his biological needs and can further his interest by sharing of historical lessons that ensure survival. Our culture and behaviors are methods to needs obtainment within our environments.

The Inner Voice of Conflict

What if wealth was the very purpose of a collective society and therefore influenced the values by which we live? *Me-conomics* makes the argument that wealth (sheep, land, money, etc...) creates the foundation of society and values help determine the methods of achieving such wealth. Without the financial benefits of working collectively, society would cease to exist and thus dissipate into chaos through constant conflict. Where differences are rooted in root value systems, differences exist of economic assumptions that further societal abrasiveness. These divergent perspectives of the rules of needs attainment that create cultural, economic, and military clashes exist. The more distant the underlying assumptions of two societies the more likely such clashes will occur.

The potential for economic clash can be seen as a function of the difference in values related to methods of needs attainment, the economic value of the transaction(s) and the anxiety level of the relationship. This can be denoted as EC=Function (DV x EV x AL) using the factors of Economic Conflict (EC), Difference of Values (DV), Economic Value (EV) and Anxiety Level (AL). This can be represented as a relationship as the following mathematical equation.

$$EC=f(DVxEVxAL)$$

Values, economics, and social strength have a large impact on organizations and their potential for success. We can see this example in executive fights over control, the spreading of rumors, employee arguments, lawsuits and even in testy union relations. What is not seen is how these factors can influence resistance type behaviors in employees that impact the overall success of the organization. When organizations create unnecessary conflicts through underdeveloped social skills, unproductive conversations, confusing expectations, and inappropriate methods of resource attainment it detracts from the success and profits of the entire entity.

A common example experienced in many organizations is that two managers are vying for the same position with limited growth potential within the organization. Their value systems are different, additional compensation is of high interest, and each has been spreading rumors about the other. As these factors begin to rise, so does the potential for conflict. Yet having clearly understood expectations for the promotion and accurate feedback appraisals will afford a greater opportunity to avoid such conflicts. In a properly run ethical organization the two employees would understand that poor behavior, unnecessary conflict, and rumor dropping would lessen their chances for economic gain of obtaining the new position or additional resources.

In the context of business, the alignment of values management, employees and the wider corporate culture should seek to be in homeostasis with the basic values of society. Where dissonance of values, economic value, and anxiety levels are high there is likely to be higher levels of internal fighting which slows down the efficient operations of the organization. Continually developing shared vantage points through training, management style, compensation and organizational structure can lessen the likelihood of potential conflict.

Another is a macro-economic approach to this model. Two nations with inherently different cultures are seeking the same resource that is necessary for their potential future success. One could use an example of scarce resource like oil in modern times or gold in the past. Such commodities could be anything of significant value to both parties. The differences in value systems, the immediate and long-term value of the commodity, as well as the anxiety level of the public and negative interactions could create a potentially explosive situation where conflict is perceived to be the solution.

Labor and management should attempt to reduce conflict and increase collaboration around core principles that benefit both themselves and society. Alignment of values throughout the entire societal network creates national efficiency in much the same way that it does within organizations. At its very root, a society, should maintain standard ethical principles that apply universally among members if homeostasis is hoped to be achieved.

Social Information Network

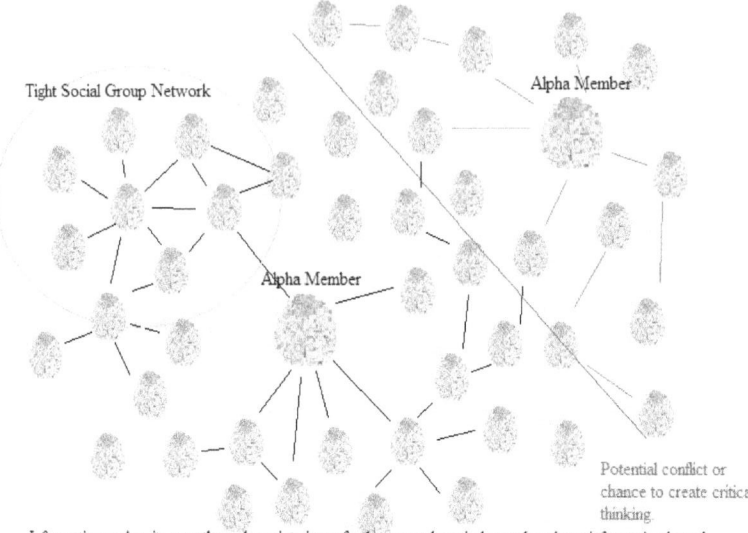

Information makes its way through society imperfectly as members judge and evaluate information based upon self-interest. This information spreads through networks. Alpha members seek influence through promoting certain beliefs, values, ideologies, and methods.

To see how overcoming conflict can lead to newer ways of thinking and greater potentials for organizational and national development can be beneficial. A conversation took place in 1550 AD in Valadolid, Spain over the human soul that sparked the invention of the greatest nation the world has ever seen. Bartolome de las Casas and Juan Gines de Sepulveda were discussing whether or not Native Americans had souls and should be considered fellow human beings. A document entitled On the Indies by the University of Salamanca postulated that Native Americans had souls and that conquest was unjustified. Las Casa stated that Native Americans were, *"...such gentleness and decency that they are, more than the other nations of the entire world, supremely*

fitted and prepared to abandon the worship of idols and to accept,

province by province and people by people, the word of God and

the preaching of the truth (Hill, 2010, p. 135). According to

Charles Hill, the author of Grand Strategies, it was such

discussions that brought to light in European minds that the world

was a larger place and that new strategies for managing it were

needed (2010). Through time and shared understandings of a new

value system does the concept of systematic administration of

multi-cultural backgrounds under a single system takes hold.

This administrative system that applies to everyone's self-

interest becomes a new vantage point. Adam Smith argued that the

wealth of nations is drawn from labor and its ability to produce

beneficial outputs. In this view, man creates all wealth and

therefore he obtains wealth through productive work. Thus, nations

earn capital by putting to progressive use the chain of labor all the

way down to the shepherd and the one that sows that grass that

feeds the flock. Society is an economic system whereupon shared

values and trust related perspectives are the fundamental glue that

holds the economic chain together. When value systems and shared perspectives break down the economic chain also begins to break down. This occurs when multiple value systems define competing and often conflicting methods of obtaining needs gratification. A nation must stand from a similar root value system if shared perspectives are to encourage unified growth that raises societal living standards.

National value systems are codified into the legal system that maintain and ethical root throughout society. Even with legal backing these value systems are strengthened by economic activity which determine how members associate for personal financial gain and the social expectations established by group activity for needs fulfillment. Without financial incentives, there will not be strong enough pressure to maintain the system's values. When collective value systems are inherently different there is likely to be a different economic systems at work and thus higher opportunities for clash. Such divergent competing ideologies can destroy innovation and efficiency within organizations and nations while overcoming challenges can develop an environment to foster it.

Philosophical Economics

Take a look to history to give us a better perspective how Americans developed their philosophical values and economic vantage points. It is through this history of intellectual development that the nature of man and society has framed the understanding of itself. More importantly these philosophical underpinnings help define the purpose of society and its economic values. These values help to define how both an organization within society and society itself should operate.

Before the modern era, economic gain was viewed from a different vantage point. The idea of personal gain would have been foreign to ancient Egyptians, Greeks, Romans, and other medieval cultures (Heilbroner, 1999). Stephan Shannon, a professor in Theoretical Archeology at the UCL Institute of Archeology, states that before modern economics, *"We engage in exchanges to make some sort of profit; they do so in order to cement social relationships; we trade in commodities; they gave gifts"*(Ridley, 2012, p. 133). The Renaissance was an era that helped people put in perspective a new mental approach that allowed merchants to gain power over the divine rights of royalty. Without this transformation in society, modern economics would still not exist. It would still be a subordinate to religious perspectives and lineage. Society would still be controlled for the benefit of the king, mullah and dictator patriarchal structure allowing for very little personal or national growth without conquest.

This is why understanding our historical past helps us in defining our economic present and future. Often these concepts come through our philosophical past where new thoughts and ideas have influenced the mental schemas that make up modern thought which further determines how people make meaning from their environment in order to fulfill their needs. Furthermore, understanding of these assumptions helps us to put in context the way in which society moves and develops toward a meaningful and beneficial future.

J. S. Mills, the author on modern concepts of liberty and freedom of speech, wrote in the 19th century how society is built from laws and customs that define distribution of wealth:

...mankind, individually or collectively, can do with them as they please. They can place them at the disposal of whomsoever they please, and on whatever terms ...Even what a person has

produced by his individual toil, unaided by anyone, he cannot keep, unless by permission of society. Not only can society take from him, but individuals could and would take it from him, if society…did not…employ pay people for the purpose of preventing him from being disturbed in possession. The distribution of wealth, therefore, depends on the laws and customs of society. The rules by which it is determined are what the opinions and feelings of the ruling portion of the community make them, and are very different in different ages and countries, and might be still more different, if mankind so chose…(Mill, 1848).

Under this concept, society determines the laws of collective living and the rules of distribution based upon underlying principles of life in that society. Thus, a man cannot keep the fruit of his labor unless society has some protection to let him do so. In the capitalistic system, man should be free to produce and keep without any unfair treatment by the power of politics; whether it is business or labor. It is this freedom to create and produce that affords workers the opportunity to develop and grow for their own best interest and for the best interest of society. According to J. S. Mill Society is in a constant state of development through the power of the mind and the development of ideas that create higher degrees of freedom.

This freedom we partially experience today started many years ago in Europe by a philosopher named John Locke. In his Second Treatise of Government (1690) which were derived from the Magna Carta and eventually led to the Bill of Rights (Hill, 2010). It is this Bill of Rights that helped Americans find a root vantage point for both personal living and the economic system. It ensures that every person should experience life, freedom and property. In the United States this has been adjusted to the environment and has become the concepts of life, liberty and the pursuit of happiness. Each person is free to think and act in ways that are for their best interest as long as these interests do not injure another person and do not conflict with the needs of society.

An economist named John Maynard Keynes believed that the strength of ideas could temper even mad men drunk off power. Even when such men hold great heights in society, their self-interest can be tempered by the encroachment of ideas. As new ideas form, it changes the dynamics and context by which people understand and exist. This is one reason why the intelligentsias are irreplaceably important in developing new ways of thinking and more accurate methods of perceiving the economic environment. These men change and push societal growth through freethinking and theorizing on where society is heading and how it is going to get there. It is this perpetual growth of thoughts that parallels the development of society; one cannot exist without the other.

One such example of an ideal that had profound impact is Niccolo Machiavelli who lived the beginning of his life in Florence under Medici until 1498 where he decided to move to Savonarola. Upon the fall of Savonarola, Machiavelliwas awarded the post of secretary to the second chancery in the Florentine democracy. Through his experience, he commented in the publication Discourses that, "*as the observance of divine institutions is the cause of the greatness of republics, so the disregard of them produces their ruin; unless it be sustained by the fear of the prince, which may temporarily supply the want of religion.*" (Bronowski&Mazlish, 1960, p. 34) In modern times, the separation of church and state, a construct of Machiavelli, developed the concept of fear of the prince, which is the rule of law and ethical standards. If the long-time traditions of divine human values are not continued, then there must be a supplemental rule of law to hold society together. In *me-conomics* it is the use of important ethical underpinnings codified by law and the socialization process that allows everyone to "know the rules of the game" which frees members of society to find ways of fulfilling their needs. Without these basic assumptions worker, managers, economic systems, and society itself will have multiple competing interests, which damage the overall development toward a justified end.

Adam Smith argues, *"The man whose whole life is spent in performing a few simple operations, of which the effects are perhaps are always the same, or very nearly the same, has no occasion to exert his understanding to exercise his invention in finding out expedients for removing difficulties which never occur"*(Bronowski&Mazlish, 1960, p. 349). Human kind must be pushed to succeed and develop by being actively engaged in the development of society. It is an ethical imperative to develop employees and laborers to higher forms of production and existence. Humans must overcome, develop, create, and innovate to solve problems in order to help develop themselves, contribute to society, and develop something spectacular. *Me-conomics* is about changing the perception of workers and their understanding of their economic systems so they can produce and have more fulfilling lives. They must know where they stand and where they can contribute to create synergy. Yet, humankind must also have a value system and rules of law to guide them in the appropriate paths that are most beneficial for everyone.

It is these rules, values, laws and methodologies that help man know where and how to find "butter for his bread". When these rules and values compete too widely or follow different assumptions there is likely to be chaos and eventually a destructive end. A singular vantage point based in self-actualization and ethical business standards will reduce the conflicting results of competing ideologies. Organizations should seek to develop higher levels of alignment with societal values in order to provide further reinforcement and strength that will foster national growth.

Interestingly, the basic values offered in religion and ethics have a benefit for society. It may be an order versus chaos type of debate but contributes to overall understanding of human development. A study of 67 countries found that those who believed in a punishment of hell versus the often-forgiving God had lower societal crime rates (Bartlett, 2012). What is important in this study is not the religious debate but the discussion of values and accountability as an influential aspect of societal living. Where separate of church and state exist, common basic ethical values and accountability must go hand-in-hand. It is through these concepts of justice, ethics and accountability that people can weigh and balance their options when considering taking the merits of illegal activities or improving their performance.

The philosopher Aristotle believed that the greatest ethical standard of business occurs when business leaders 1.) exercise the virtue of prudence and wisdom and 2.) the philosophical search for truth (Bragues, 2006). Under these concepts, the greatest ethical imperative is for businesses to allow people to actively engage in the management of the business and contemplate the meaning of their environment. Thus, employees become actively engaged in the overall success of the organization when they have influence on it and feel responsible for it. *Me-conomics* helps encourage ethical behavior within strong innovative and efficient practices that both fits within the capitalistic approach and can potentially spawn a new economic vantage point that drives economic growth and worker loyalty. Through both individualist and collective engagement in the economy, organizations can create market advantages by aligning the individual parts to meet environmental threats.

The Counter Communist Perspective

At times it is beneficial to look at the counter perspective to capitalism to see how well the principles worked in the economic environment. One economic vantage point that maintained a promise to level the inequalities in society but ultimately failed in its experiment was communism. In the communistic perspective, all men work together and reap the same rewards. This is a very noble idea that has little practical utility on a larger scale. The concept worked well within the commune where individual accountability existed in the small group context but failed to live up to its ideal on a multinational scale where market participants did not know each other. Communism lacks the ability to take into account the innate need for humans to develop and master their environments for personal need.

The problems associated with communism lay in its close association with a perfectly ordered society where everyone has a defined place of contribution. The fallacy in this concept is people cannot be more than that societal place by which they are already defined leaving little enthusiasm to innovate either themselves or their environment. Communism in the Soviet Union eventually crashed because the masses no longer were motivated to work for an ideal or a handful of breadcrumbs. It was a huge national expense to keep the system operating thereby accumulating huge deficits. They had no method of sparking innovative effort within their system and thus forced to move into an arena of corruption, as a significant method of individual needs fulfillment. To satisfy their needs outside of the theoretical understanding of the communist system means an eventual death to the system. The same threat exists equally in capitalism, socialism or communism when people are forced to find different illegal and often unethical methods of fulfilling their needs. Capitalism and *me-conomics* encourages needs attainment of the masses through freedom and personal development. In such situations, laws and culture provide structure but man is relatively free within these positive societal constraints to develop and reap the rewards of his labor. Capitalism should be about guiding humans to self-actualization and allowing them and their organizations to share in the benefits.

The Communist Manifesto swept through the world as a backlash against the abuses of kings, dictators, underdeveloped republics, and the old order (Heilbroner, 1999). Karl Marx and Fridrich Engels wrote the work for the concept of collective and mutually beneficial society. In most places of Europe, the ideas were rejected wholesale except in Russia and China where some form or another were adapted and customized. Yet both authors recognized that the communist principle must eventually end and the experiment would fail. This is what precisely happened when the Soviet Union collapsed. The rigid rules of a perfectly ordered society could not stand against the winds of change. There simply was no innovation, motivation or satisfaction to keep society together or overcome market challenges.

Charles Darwin believed that, "*it is not the strongest species that survive, not the most intelligent, but most responsive to change*" (Gilley, Thompson, &Gilley, 2012). Economic systems die, are destroyed or replaced because they failed to adjust and take account of human needs or the changing of times. The Industrial Revolution and the American Revolution are testimony to the belief that societies must innovate to find additional resources for success. The purpose of economics is not the creation of wealth alone but also includes the commerce of societal development. In the case of communism, societal development was muted by excessive control. Capitalism allows people to develop together in order to push for growth and adjust when the market demands it. When and if a people loose trust in a system or the system is not in alignment with global, nationalistic, and individual needs the system will be replaced by that which is more willing to change. It is a Darwinian adapt or die mentality!

President Herbert Hoover stated, "*Economic depression cannot be cured by legislative action or executive pronouncement. Economic wounds must be healed by the action of the cells of the economic body-the producers and consumers themselves*". Society develops based upon the development of the foundation of the economic system, which rests within individual workers, and the organizations that develop pathways for worker success. The more successful the individual, the more successful society becomes.

The approach of the economic system should rest in the development of individuals in order to create the highest levels of both personal and national development.

The Individual and the Collective

Threats to the capitalistic system are present today as they have been in the past. A Depression era economist Joseph Schumpeter believed the biggest threat to the U.S. was stagnation of growth (Heilbroner, 1999). Capitalism must continuously expand and grow to be an effective player in world markets. To him once innovation has been replaced by bureaucratic control the economy will become less effective, which in turn causes a decline in new ideas, products, and markets.

President Franklin D. Roosevelt further sheds light on the connection of individual and collective impact, "*In our personal ambitions we are individualists. But in our seeking for economic and political progress as a nation, we all go up or else we all go down as one people.*" In society, people are naturally connected to each other and feed off each other's ideas in synergistic fashion. The rules of society need to ensure a level playing field with accountability for all members if new businesses are to development, people are to grow, and the economic system to expand.

Questioning how business is conducted is important for maintaining the momentum of societal growth. Innovation and efficiency comes from the sparking of new ideas that encourage economic growth. Those who are not in knowledge, do not seek to gain knowledge, or ponder the nature of knowledge are hindering societal growth by blocking the natural desires of individuals to succeed. The power of employee innovation and efficiency can be great if harnessed and guided through ethical leadership. Questioning the nature and processes of businesses helps in fostering more efficient methods of understanding and helps to ensure higher levels of ethical development. Ignorance is the enemy of a free thinking nation. Rene Descartes, a French Philosopher of the 16th Century believed, *"I shall consider myself as having no hands, no eyes, no flesh, no blood, nor any senses; yet falsely believing myself to possess all these things. If, by this means, it is not in my power to arrive at the knowledge of any truth, I may at least do what is in my power, namely suspend judgment, and thus avoid belief in anything false and avoid being imposed upon by this arch deceiver, however powerful and deceptive He may be* (Bronowski & Mazlish, 1960, p. 223)."

Rene Descartes described how ignorance is the worst fallacy for those who are making judgments. This ignorance can be seen in employees low productivity levels, supervisory chest pounding, executive turf wars, government leaders engaging in excessive party politics, investor's narrow focus on short-term stock price with no balance of long-term needs. This self-focused and shortsighted viewpoint that creates layers of mismanagement in business and government. Without realigning the needs of societal membership and its roots values, it is likely that the short sighted disintegration of a country will continue.

Worse than ignorance alone is ignorance and power combined. Christopher Columbus, one of the discoverers of this New World, understood the power of money. Columbus believed, *"Those who has gold makes and accomplishes whatever he wishes in the world and finally uses it to send souls to paradise."* His belief was that money and power can change the very nature of society and determine the values of human life. However, laws should supersede the rules of finance by focusing on long-term objectives of society improvement versus shortsighted economic interests. Through a proper balance of current needs and long-term growth the system moves more towards alignment and development.

One can find an example where the rule of law, ethics, and common sense broke down. An investigation of market manipulation in Europe indicated that a potential ring leaders at Barclay's had a circle/network of associates at Credit Agricole, HSBC, Deutsche Bank and SocieteGenerale (Guthrie, 2012). A Euroswap trader by the name of Philippe Moryoussef appeared to have connections to other banks through employment jumping associates creating a network of self-enrichment. Moryoussef sent out messages to a number of members highlighting the creation of specific eras of manipulation. Groups like this and their associated banks shared both financial and value-laden perspectives that created many years of market manipulation. The end result of similar type activity was the longest economic recession in history and inaccurate labor rate manipulation that impacted everything from student loans to government financing. If this were true we would know the larger system has inefficiencies because there is compelling reasons for the members to choose unethical behavior over more productive ones. This creates both a value system and an incentive for working outside the system. Thus, underlying member logic has been manifesting itself in the group's decisions that find the benefit of reward more compelling than risk of discovery, fines or prosecution. The more common such activities become the more risk to the synergistic pieces that fuel the capitalistic system. Furthermore, decisions by a few impacted the global market creating difficulties for hundreds of millions of people.

The economy is a large system with many different components all connected to each other. When the economic system is at risk it has parasitic elements bent on self-gain outside of the common value systems the nation holds. A risk of financial, moral, and personal collapse occurs when such networks have the power to impact the reality and understandings within the economic system. Adam Smith stated, *"Human society, when we contemplate it in a certain and abstract and philosophical light, appears like a great, an immense machine whose regular and harmonious movements produce a thousand agreeable effects"*

(Bronowski&Mazlish, 1960, p. 352). Society is like a machine whereby the misalignment of economic assumptions destroys innovation and efficiency through detraction and unethical manipulation. Bankers to laborers need to be on the same page in order to create high levels of motivation, innovation, satisfaction to further development. One cannot take unfairly from the other. We must all see our lives without blindness to the possibilities of a higher form of existence. The failure of developing a well-greased machine with similar vantage points is to stagnate the economy by delaying required maintenance. Eventually the machine will putter to its end or be superseded by a more productive system that moves back into homeostasis.

As the path, the authors of the Declaration of Independence believed in a free government where everyone can reap from the fruits of their labor without tyrannical molestation. Thomas Jefferson wrote, "*A wise and frugal Government, which shall restrain men from injuring one another, shall leave them otherwise free to regulate their own pursuits of industry and improvement and shall not take from the mouth of labor the bread it has earned. This is the sum of good government, and this is necessary to close the circle of our felicities"* (Bronowski&Mazlish, 1960, p. 390). In order to spark an innovative revolution in the American economy the enlightenment of freedom of thought, economic gain, and pursuit of happiness needs to be fostered. Thomas Jefferson further postulated, *"I have sworn upon the altar of God eternal hostility against every form of tyranny over the mind of man."*

A nation must create the right mix between innovation (EF), motivation through rewards from the economic system (ER), in the pursuit of happiness (ES) in order to balance the necessary ingredients for success to continue to perpetuate society forward. Nations need new ideas, proper economic rewards, and the possibility of finding homeostasis in their daily existence for both political stability and future viability. Where these factors are not in alignment the system will be missing key components and will likely be dysfunctional; if not tyrannical.

This tyranny can come in many different forms. Adam Smith believed in the invisible hand of market action whereby those nations most able to produce new products and services are most likely to succeed on the global market. Tyranny influences methodology and avenues by which people obtain their wealth from the economic system. Smith also believed that when the invisible hand has been manipulated it distorts the market's influence by creating an unfair and inefficient system (Jones, 2007). Economic development only works if the public good, higher levels of human capital, and needs obtainment are found through free and fair market competition that allows individuals to work in their self-interest. When unmolested markets no longer work it requires ever higher levels of oversight and cost in order to ensure the system is running smoothly. If homeostasis cannot be maintained the system begins to decline in strength due to the weight of its own maintenance.

The Changing Economic System

Skeptics do not necessarily believe that systems adjust, change, and redevelop at new stages. This bias is based in limited understanding as a result of focusing only on one's limited lifetime and not having a historical perspective of society. Each major war was a result of two different visions competing for influence and thus creating their own economic realities. To see how the economic system changes and transforms we can again look to one of the more prominent philosophers at the end of World War I (WWI).

John Maynard Keynes once wrote, *"It is for this reason that a decline in money values so severe as that which we are now experiencing threatens the solidity of the whole financial structure. Banks and bankers are by nature blind"* (1963, p. 176). Keynes further described financial life at the end of WWI as, *"In many countries bankers are becoming unpleasantly aware of the fact that, when their customers' margins have run off, they are themselves 'on margin'. I believe that, if to-day a really conservative valuation were made of all the doubtful assets, quite a significant proportion of the banks of the world would be found to be insolvent..."* (1963, p. 177). During this time a transformation of the banking system, the gold standard, and societal structure were in rapid transition. Society lost faith in the aristocratic system and its financial network. A number of countries were plundered and destroyed... and the world changed!

Economic theories, and the success of nations, are based deeply in their explanation of behavioral science and psychological development. Alan Greenspan argued in the book The Age

of Turbulence: Adventures in a New World that, *"if the economy*
could be accurately modeled using empirical facts and math, then
large-scale forecasts could be derived methodically, without the
quasi-scientific intuition by so many economic forecasters" (2008,
p. 36). Greenspan stated that economic systems change frequently
enough that is it difficult to find accurate models by which to make
strong forecasts. *Me-conomics* moves to deeper human data points
that rest at the core of time constrained economic systems to help
balance predictions of economic development based upon the
logical thought construction of society. When new thoughts and
innovations hit the market, the world spins again and so does the
economic model. Therefore, looking deeply into human nature will
tell us why such phenomenon occurs. It is an attempt to remove the
veil from economic understandings within individuals,
organizations, cultures, and economies. To develop a theory and
model to see the unseen vantage points based on economic
approaches for needs attainment embedded in the very existence of
social life. Nations that can best harness the power of the human
brain are likely to find the greatest level of innovation, social and
economic development.

A new view of the economy is needed during this period of global and economic integration. Thomas Mun, the director of the East India Company, stated in England's Treasure by Foreign Trade around 1630 that the normal means by which a nation increases its wealth is through trade, *"wherein we must ever observe this rule; to sell more strangers yearly than we consume of theirs in value"* (Heilbroner, 1995, p. 40). To him the economic system was relatively simple. A nation that desires to earn more income need only sell more than it buys regardless of the details of how this occurs. Yet, times have changed and the system has spread its economic vines the world over creating complex financial patterns that connect and reconnect at many locations.

In today's world, the economic system has become much more complex and such simple definitions are no longer adequate. Where products are sold, people must have the capital to buy those products creating a world of interconnected laborers and companies. As the global middle class increases, it will be those nations that have the ability to harness the power of innovation and efficiency to solve global product and service problems that will be able to maintain their global positions. The race to the top is really more of a race to develop the human mind to new ways of thinking about topics and issues. It is about harnessing this power in new, unique and synergist manners to provide globally relevant products and services. This requires a global minded leadership that can understand the wide structural foundations of business and government.

Chapter One Conclusions

Decision-making should be filtered through a process that helps leaders understand the wider network of context as well as limit the potential bias associated with such decisions. Poor decisions can have a significant impact on the viability of America's economy 10, 15, or 20 years from now. Furthermore, organizational leaders have a responsibility to encourage the development of workers in order to encourage the development of society, the organization, and the individual. Such decisions can be difficult without a methodology to weigh often-conflicting opportunities. Through the *me-conomic* principles and decision filters, leaders are better able to weigh and judge their decisions. Society, science and history has provided some frameworks for understanding and developing methodology that when used together provide a stronger framework for decision-making and understanding of world reality. Decisions should be filtered through the following concepts:

1.) History/Vision: The U.S. started with a vision of the founders based upon certain principles and values rooted in pursuit of happiness and liberty. These principles and values are where decisions should be centered in order to ensure proper anchoring of ideas and furthering of the national vision.

2.) Religious/Ethical/Philosophical: Concepts and new ideas help ensure a more ethical world, which fosters societal growth and peace. Such decisions should encourage and support fair and just treatment of individuals in society. The legal system should be the neutral party that enforces these underlying ethical commerce rules.

3.) Science and Logic: Decisions should be based in the logical deductions of science, evidence, and pragmatism. Understanding both the arguments for and against a decision helps to foster critical thinking. Leaders should be *open minded* to the concept that the way they think today may not be the only viable answer and could be damaging

the chances of their kinsman.

Chapter 2
Employee Reality Construction
Ab Esse Ad Posse Valet Consequentia
(Since it is Real it is Possible!)

Ab Esse Ad Posse Valet Consequentia

Since it is Real it is Possible!

"The 'real world' is to a large extent unconsciously built upon the language habits of the group. The worlds in which different societies live are **distinct** *worlds, not merely the same world with different labels attached. We see and hear and otherwise experience very largely as we do because the language habits of our community predispose certain choices of interpretation"*(Sapir, 1929).

It is precisely the choice of language use that creates a level of understanding that differs from nation-to-nation and person-to-person. Yet those within the same group should share relatively the same understandings of society, based upon shared experiences, in order to develop stronger economic networks with greater ability to obtain resources and fulfill the needs of its members. In Western thought the categories of space, time causation, numbers and personhood influence people's understandings of their environments (Hollis & Lukes, 1982). These understandings change based upon what place in history people are in and the cultural lens by which they make meaning from their environment.

Reality is the *"appertaining to phenomena that we recognize as having a being independent of our own volition (i.e. we cannot wish them away) and to define 'knowledge'" as the certainty that phenomena are real and that they possess specific characteristics"* (Berger & Luckman, 1966, p. 1). Reality is that which we physically cannot deny and the phenomena of understanding which we interpret as knowledge. Most members of society have a basic understanding of the physical reality but make different meaning from this based upon their cultural understandings. This culture impacts the perceptions and vantage points of workers as they make basic understandings of their work environment.

Society and workers can make all types of different understandings of their environment that are not always logical or beneficial for their needs. Nietzsche developed a concept of "false consciousness" that can lead to the deception of man, the deception of self, and contribute to false assumptions about the world (Kaufmann, 1956). These irrational beliefs are based in all types of environmental understandings as they seek resources, power, or wealth. In most cases, society tells people what to believe and this may not always be the ultimate truth or a motivating component of life. When a culture has socialized others to unproductive beliefs it can take a devastating toll on an organization and the economy at large as these concepts expand into an institutional order.

"And because he who enlists a man's mind wields a power even greater than the sword or the scepter, these men shaped and swayed the world" (Heilbroner, 1999, p. 13).

Beliefs are often institutionalized across society as subjective 'truths'. Institutionalization is the process of coming to an alignment of common meaning with others in society. Whenever three or more people are in a room they will inevitably communicate until all members share similar vantage points and perspectives. Workers in organizations also engage in the institutionalization process bringing in contextual information from previous processes based in their upbringing and experience. When these institutions (concepts/expectations) become the norm they begin to perpetuate themselves in an expanding institutional order that encourages workers to believe in their constructed meaning (Berger & Luckman, 1966). For example, members of labor unions will begin to adopt and accept the basic values of their labor parties and perpetuate them while believing that they are truly theirs. It would take significant social pressure, logical alternatives, and a new environment to change their assumptions about the benefits or detractors of being part of this political and social network.

Vantage Points and Reasoning

In order to make effective business decisions based in strong logic it is beneficial to understand how our individual concepts of reality creates a vantage point that biases our most basic beliefs. For example, the concept of relativism entails the understanding that knowledge is based upon persons, places, culture and history. It is a relativist understanding that each person and culture experiences their own understanding of their environment. The relativist doctrine indicates (Hollis &Lukes, 1982):

1.) the observation that the beliefs on a certain topic can be different;

2.) that beliefs are found within contextual situations and are relative to the circumstances of the user.

Each person has a particular vantage point by which they understand their beliefs and make meaning of their world. Even though we share a physical world with everyone else we do not necessarily share the same understandings of that world. Language helps us understand and make meaning from our environments. Schlick believed that the very meaning of a sentence is its method of verification (Schlick, 1936). Through this understanding it is possible to envision how words are representations of experience. They only have meaning if we share a level of collective understanding that makes language possible.

In such a situation the different uses of language can often denote a different reality in understanding. For example, executives often use different language and symbolism than factory workers. Likewise, farmers will use different language symbols people from the city. It is this language that helps us understand the differences in reality construction. Analyzing language can help us determine a groups root assumptions about their 'quality world' and make appropriate predictions.

Some may call these assumptions a vantage point or a schema. It is possible to pick out employees environmental assumptions and vantage points by focusing on these true sentences. Such true sentences are the themes that lead back to basic assumptions and values the employee holds. By doing so it is possible to understand the reality, or meaning making, the employee is using. To do so well through active listening can help managers adjust their environments to bring employees into a proper perspective of organizational expectations and make daily decisions that help both the company and themselves.

The use of language helps us define a concept called a stream of consciousness. The stream of consciousness is the way in which people put together pictures and images to create an understanding of their environment (Edelman & Tononi, 2010). It is this stream of consciousness that is used to understand and make meaning from the environment. Culture, religion, language, past experiences, and present experiences are connected together to try and understand the environment in which we live. This understanding is our reality.

A number of considerations that leaders should understand when trying to understand both their own and their employees' rationality. The considerations are as follows (Hollis &Lukes, 1982):

1.) Different styles of reasoning exist based in our history and change over the course of a life.

2.) Reasoning can be substantiated with true or false conclusions.

3.) The possibilities of true or false conclusions are based upon historical events that determine what type of reasoning are used.

4.) Categories of possible answers exist.

5.) People have difficulties judging the reasoning values of other people because they are not independent or mutually exclusive.

Employees and decision makers often come from different backgrounds, vantage points, reasoning skills, and usage of language. These different vantage points and understandings create differences in the type of reasoning and logic skills utilized. A manager may be explaining something that makes perfect logical sense to him but may have very little logical meaning for the employee. Understanding the varying perspectives and how each side understands these concepts creates additional opportunities for alignment of word and message.

These realities are rooted in of knowledge which can be further derived from reason, custom, imagination, and history. Thus, people who base their decisions solely on custom and imagination do not necessarily know a concept in depth because they are limited by quick bias without adequate analysis. Truth must be judged against the physical facts of the world and based in logical beliefs. The concepts of causality of events, impartiality of beliefs, symmetry of explanation, and reflexivity of study help us be more accurate in our thinking (Hollis & Lukes, 1982).

Changing Beliefs

It is not easy for people to change the way they think or what they believe; nor is it easy for them to change the way others believe. A radical departure from the institutionalized truth creates resistance among members. People are confined by the adopted framework for understanding both current and future issues. All new concepts are put within the context of older concepts and methodologies. Each builds on the other but does not necessarily change those root assumptions. The very language group members use to define their reality confines them to certain beliefs and understandings. Language and its use in cognitive processes helps people define what they deem as their reality (Berger & Luckman, 1966). To change reality often relies on changing language and its root assumptions.

Language then becomes a depository of gaining new information and fits within the cohesive whole without reconstructing the entire order of thinking (Goffman, 1963). New information is added to older information; layering on top of each other. Each new type of information continually defines older information but does not necessarily change how it is organized or managed within a person's mind or social group. Many organizational problems can be related to how organizations fail to gain a level of new understanding of their world and how they fit within it.

Most people can learn on a couple of different levels. In the first place they can learn through pain and pleasure in a hedonistic lifestyle. This is a stimulus-response type of automatic learning seen in animals. However, when stimulus and response develop into more complex concepts a higher form of learning occurs that changes beliefs and perceptions (Tolman, 1932). This type of higher order is thinking that helps people define the world in which they live.

Those beliefs that are rooted in one's social group or testimony alone may not necessarily be rational by nature. The belief can simply be social constructions based in understandings of human life and behavior that are not realized in the physical world. For example, a unionized environment derived from members of a particular social class might view the world of work distinctly different than those from the upper echelons of society. The socialization aspects, as derived in *me-conomics*, may impact and adjust the principles of meaning making through rational environmental adjustments. Thus the rules of society that we hold to be true are based in the multitude of actors who hold the same beliefs and reinforce them through social pressure. If these beliefs are challenged and overcome by new beliefs then new realities can be formed which impact the way we view the world.

As new information is presented and greater understanding occurs people make meaning from a variety of sources. This may be religion, government, laws, social networks, work networks, skills, etc… to synthesize the information into a concrete whole understanding (Berger & Luckman, 1966). According to Durkheim sociology this cohesive whole is an attempt to make meaning from their environment in a way that helps them to understand how to make predictions on how to act, work, and exist in the future. These conceptually blended beliefs and methods of needs fulfillment becomes their new role in work and society.

Chaos of Change: Will to Power

Roles are part of our process of the social self. When new arguments, manners of thinking, and views become apparent there is a level of chaos created. Yet, once these ideas are settled, there is something called habituation that occurs. Habituation is responding less to the change in an environment as it takes on a new normal. Learned activities (i.e., new organizational approaches) become ritualized to save people from spending too much personal energy. It becomes a new way of acting or role-playing in the environment.

Given the historical accumulation of knowledge in a society, we can assume that because of the division of labor role-specific knowledge will grow at a faster rate than generally relevant and accessible knowledge. The multiplication of specific tasks brought about by the division of labor requires standardized solutions that can be readily learned and transmitted. These in turn require specialized knowledge of certain situations, and of the means/ends relationships in terms of which the situations are socially defined. In other words, specialists will arise, each of whom will have to know whatever is deemed necessary for the fulfillment of his particular task (Berger & Luckmann, 1966, p. 77).

When there is no competing information to current beliefs people will perpetuate existing allocations of labor and work roles. Employees, managers, and executives live and foster these roles both within their own and others social classes. An employee will act and be subordinate in the same way that an executive will act and expect to make decisions. These role related behaviors allow for society to maintain order but also comes with the price of stagnated individual development within organizations and the nation. To develop an organization requires some changes in stereotyped behavior between management and employees.

The role of labor and its particular vantage point is often based in an individual's perception and educational achievement. When a considerable amount of time and effort has been exhausted in a specific employment arena, it becomes difficult for an employee to develop in other areas (Roe, 1956). Thus, the amount of time, wealth and energy available for other pursuits limits the ability of employees to also develop new self-concepts and social networks. It is these particular vantage points that leaders should try and understand in order to see problems from employee's perspectives.

These perspectives are based in symbolism of thoughts, ideas, self-perception and culture. The universe of people is based in the symbolic nature of our existence and the world in which we exist. Workers make meaning through their memory which is drawn from individual socialization within society. Throughout their lives workers derive the meaning of their work through their associated memories of whom they are and where they are. The interpretation of these memories defines their very existence. If a construction worker came from a family of construction workers, he/she may associate construction work with connection to family history and purpose. It will be difficult for this person to change their root assumptions about themselves or the habits they use to fulfill their needs in the world.

When people have a common set of beliefs they have some foundation for coming to a similar understanding of the environment. Managers and employees should seek to create this commonality for higher levels of development and understanding. Engagement comes from the ability to create mutual understanding in a constant negotiation of understanding. Before such mutual understanding occurs it is important for managers to understand that employee's logic and understanding that it is as true for the employees as it is for the managers.

"...take it as given that most beliefs are correct. The reason for this is that a belief is identified by its location in a pattern of beliefs; it is what the belief is about. Before some object in, or aspect of, the world can become part of the subject-matter of a belief (truth or false) there must be endless true beliefs about the subject matter" (Davidson, 1975, p. 20).

As people move up the social ranks in society, they have greater opportunities to influence others understandings of reality. For example, a chief of a tribe can set the rules within his tribe and over time these rules begin to define the very existence and nature of that tribe. The way tribal members think, solve issues, and approach issues is defined by the norms, values, and beliefs as presented by a chieftain. The more people who accept those beliefs the more they are embedded and perpetuated into the collective conscious of that tribe. The world around them changes as their understandings change. The same process applies when managers become executives and can create greater influence on their environment and used institutional factors to perpetuate beliefs.

Research conducted by Liu, Liao & Loi (2012) on the automobile teams in a large Midwestern car manufacturer helps highlight this key point. They found that abusive executives perpetuated their own order or understanding of the environment. Through the modeling of their behavior lower level managers began to adopt their characteristics and perpetuate these perceptions on to their employees. Employees either complied with such behavior or resisted them. Such negativity and poor perception damaged employee's creative abilities leaving them less able to contribute to organizational solutions. Such reality formation took a cascading effect throughout the organization and eventually stifled innovation, motivation, and satisfaction.

To move against such a reality means great pain and suffering. To Nietzche, the Will to Power is the ultimate need of every man to influence his environment but only a few can do with high levels of volition. It is the constant seeking to influence, control and develop oneself in the context of society that creates this transformation of mind and spirit. To move against such institutional orders and power structures means to think for yourself and *will to power* on a new plane of existence reserved primarily for artists, saints, and philosophers. It is a process of painful self-actualization. Nieszche summed it up as *"I assess the power of will by how much resistance, pain, and torture it endures and knows how to turn to its advantage"* (Kaufmann, 1974, p.211). To move into a free thinking existence also means to reject what society has taught you as true and reintegrate new understandings into one's identity.

Nieszche further explained the concept of self-transformation and free thinking, *"One should…not…think little of this…phenomenon merely because it is painful…At bottom, it is…that very instinct of freedom. Only here the material upon which the form-giving and ravishing nature of this force vents itself is man himself, his…animalic…self-and not…other men. This secret self-ravishment, this artists' cruelty, this pleasure is given form to oneself as a hard, recalcitrant, suffering material-burning*

into it a will, a critique, a contradiction, a contempt, a No-

this…work of a soul that is willingly divided against itself and

makes itself suffer-the whole activistic "bad conscious" has…been

the real womb of all ideal and imaginative events and has thus

brought to light an abundance of strange new beauty and

affirmation-and perhaps beauty itself" (Kaufman, 1974, p. 253).

To see one self and reality from a clear lens requires the

ability to critically think about self and society. All embedded

information from childhood must be questioned and burnt into

something new from pain and suffering. It is to stand on one's own

feet and see the institutional order of one's socialized environment.

Yet, through the development of one's mind new methods of

finding solutions to complex problems are possible. Ultimately the

level of development and critical thinking in human attainment is

mirrored in scientific methodology. Thus, the *socialized* self falls

away to the *true* self. It is the ultimate ethical imperative of

business and government. It is a *will to power* the creative aspects

of those in society that can further societal growth while

suppressing societal elements that seek self-gain at the expense of society.

Logic of Life

Imagine for a moment you were able to put on a special body suit that captured virtually every sensation a person would obtain from their environment. Every look, action, sound, movement and characteristic of our environment was recorded without loss of detail. Once recorded it is downloaded into a computer and analyzed for patterns of behavior, meanings from conversations, and imperceptible subtle cues in response to various stimuli. You would then have an excellent understanding of the similarities in behavior that are common to most human beings. Those items that are in common would be driven by an underlying logic to life and to society. This logic is rooted in the very innate survival of the species and creates the framework and neurological connections to understand the environment no matter what culture you were raised in.

The same process applies when considering how our subconscious collects large amounts of information and begins to make meaning from that information throughout our earthly time.

The more we reflect on our lifetime learning the more likely we are able to draw out of our subconscious connections important information to use in purposeful ways that benefit our survival and goals. This is called awareness. To draw forth using basic principles learned throughout our lifetimes to truly self-actualize our goals (will to power). To the far majority of people this self-actualization occurs later in life while in some it never happens. Beyond the need for survival is the need to create homeostasis in our feelings, health, and self-perception related to the mastery of our environment. This is where *me-conomics*, or the survival of the socialized self, begins to discuss these principles for a more just and productive organizational and economic system. Those that can master their immediate needs and find important contributions to self and society can experience a freedom others only dream about. In the context of the workplace the organization and the individual can capitalize on self-actualization to create higher levels of performance.

Societal logic is that which is derived from environmental factors of cause and effect. The very reason why employees engage in certain actions is to benefit themselves the most. The logic can be derived from inductive and deductive reasoning based upon the extrapolation of individual behaviors that helps people influence their work or personal environment. The very purpose of science is to determine the why of our actions through logical and researched principles while reducing socialized bias. Using the construct of a theory helps limit this bias. A theory can be defined as an abstraction that allows people to make sense out of a large amount of facts related to an issue(s) (Blanchard & Thacker, 2010). Thus a theory is a lens to understanding. Theoretical lessons of education can give us the frame work but it is the environment that gives us the truest test of validity.

The concept of societal logic is not a new one. After the reign of King Louis XIV a historian by the name of Montesquieu wrote about historical logic. His belief can be summed in, *"those who have said that a blind fatality has produced all the effects that we see in the world uttered a great absurdity; for what greater absurdity than a blind fatality which has produced intelligent beings. Therefore, there is an **original reason**; and laws are the relations which are found between it and different beings, and the relations of these **beings among themselves"** (Bronowski &

Mazlish, 1960). In today's world we can call this

the subconscious logic and the employee behavior that manifests

from it.

Logic, and the understanding of logic, may be culturally

associated (Hollis, 1968). In the example, "p,p implies q, therefore

q" there are some associated assumptions being made. This is

stated as a *modus ponens* and could be represented as (p,

$(p\rightarrow q))\rightarrow q$. If p implies q then it is somehow associated with q.

Different types of personalities may find different relevance in this

association until there is a level of logical justification between the

two. A more exact person may desire a direct association while

someone more intuitive would need to see that they are somehow

associated in order to see the validity. Properly aligned

organizations can help in making important connections between

employee understandings and employer needs through the use of

logic.

Expanding on this concept just a bit, it may be possible to

see the differences in the subconscious logic and culturally laden

conscious logic. The subconscious logic works at a much more

pure level then the socialized conscious. Let us take the example of multiple associations in a complex arrangement in the subconscious that humans have difficulty being aware. These associations can be drawn out with learning and reflection. Such arrangements might be complex and appear as $[(p, (p{\rightarrow}q){\rightarrow}q)+(q, (q{\rightarrow}z){\rightarrow}q)]=p{\rightarrow}z$. These connections could be so long that we are looking at only shadows of logic that need to be explained or methodically joined for others to understand. Yet, it is these imprints of cause, effect, and association from multiple paths that allows us to test assumptions in our environment. This may just be one of the reasons why the highly intelligent gifted can make larger and more complex associations that are drawn out from reflection through the rational cognitive processes or having high emotional intelligence that allows one to understand the emotions used to embed the information. If an action occurs that we do not understand we may be able to trace back the result to its beginning with enough time and effort. If we are unaware we would just feel the association while awareness will allow us to draw it out and manipulated it. Employees should understand the requirements of their work environment and both logically understand and intuitively feel what the right choices of behavior are when no policies or procedures are available. Such intuitive and logical understandings would be an ultimate alignment between the organizational needs and that of the employee.

People with higher intelligence levels and greater levels of awareness can make wider and deeper connections between various events in the marketplace solving complex problems and creating both organizational and personal innovation. Inside their brains the electrical connections are greater and loss of transference of information is less due to stronger insulation and additional efficiency in connecting information (Heylighen, 2003). It is these connections and new patterns of thinking that can create new innovative ideas and efficient paths to be realized within the workplace. Removing unnecessary procedural steps that create inefficiency and confusion within organizations can increase profit margins by reducing waste, cost, and loss of time through indecision. Intelligence is often definedby the ability to solve complex abstract problems in the environment and put them to practical use. Intelligence in business has a central focus of taking conceptual ideas and turning them into new streams of revenue. Doing this on an organizational scale can move the continuum of work productivity from a lower level to a higher one.

Encouraging employees to be more innovative and productive can create its own beliefs over time. Beliefs are based in the symbolisms people learn throughout their lives. Religion, social values, employment and family can encourage accurate or inaccurate beliefs not based in logic. When employee's perceptions are rooted in symbolic meaning that helps them define their environment they may come to improper beliefs about work, their place in the world, and life. Symbolism can cause poorly constructed mechanisms where people draw a false conscious that leads to inappropriate patterns of effort. If these false beliefs become collective, they can have a devastating impact on the work environment and its financial success. When this inefficiency occurs, the symbolism can be the root of the problem in illogical thinking (Goody, 1961).

People are naturally inclined to make meaning from their environment. Workers are no exception and will take in subtle cues from their work environment and managers messages to create these beliefs. The Sapir-Whorf hypothesis indicated:

"We dissect nature along lines laid down by our native languages.

The categories and types that we isolate from the world

phenomena we do not find there because they stare every observer

in the face; on the contrary, the world is presented in a

kaleidoscopic flux of impressions which has to be organized by our

minds-and this means largely by the linguistic system in our

minds"(Whorf, 1954, p. 213).

A new science has emerged called Neuroeconomics that ties the processing of the brain to the economic decisions people make. The researchers postulate that the brain's anatomy, combined with economic models of neural activity, give new insight on how workers obtain, spend and invest money (Fischman, 2012). Dr. Colin F. Camerer, a professor in behavioral finance and economics from the California Institute of Technology believes that neuroeconomics is 90% neuroscience and 10% economics. That people are driven by the desire to maximize their own happiness and this makes its way into rational economic activity. For example, extremely low or high contractual or economic offers manifest themselves in feelings that are a result of different activation centers in the brain. Furthermore, Dr. Paul

Glimcher, the director of the Center for Neuroeconomics at New York University believes that economics, psychology, and neuroscience are making their way into a single field of study (Fishman, 2012). A strong example is offered from Dr. Ernst Fehr, a professor in economics at the University of Zurich found that those who share money have more activity in the temporo-parietal junction associated empathy while selfish people had less activation. The front of the brain, dorsolateral prefrontal cortex, is associated with deliberative thought and calculation. It is the fostering of deliberative thought and calculation that can further the success of an organization and encourage pro-social collective improvements.

Thus, pleasure and dislike are a direct result of our basic cognitive make-up. Some people are more predisposed to collaborative and mutual beneficial economic activities and there are those that are more predisposed to more negative or selfish actions. Moving to a deeper data point in understanding how and why people make the economic and business decisions they do also creates the opportunity for the encouragement of higher levels of economic activity and positive action. Organizations that desire to maximize the potential of their employees should understand how their employee's minds work and why they may decide to engage in mutually beneficial action or not engage in these actions.

To change the workplace often requires the change of perception and perspective of self, the organization, or society. The reality for most people relies heavily in the here and now (Berger &Luckman, 1966). In other terms, they are concerned with what their body needs here and what issues are presented now. Attention is very pragmatic in current problems and issues. The majority of worker intention is focused on what they are currently doing, have done in the past, and plan on doing in the very near future. Employees often use this presence to determine how current information fits within those needs. This is one of the reasons why it is difficult for managers to encourage employees to see the larger picture of their actions. Such employees are living in the present with little understanding of their greater association and connection with the wider environment. Management should always try and expand this association through historical, economic, and personal understandings that tie employees to more productive understandings and actions. This is a process of socialization through close relationships and story sharing between management and worker.

The division of labor offers an opportunity to engage in collective and individual actions that influence their environment. Impacting the environment solves problems for both the individual and the society at large. Generally, the way people perceive their role in society is deeply associated with their specific function within the overall economic system. Work provides the employee a number of important outlets for self-actualization (Vroom, 1964):

1.) Work roles provide wages to the role occupation in exchange for their services and efforts.

2.) Work requires the expenditure of mental and physical energy.

3.) Work provides an opportunity for people to engage in the production of goods and services.

4.) Work provides the role occupant an opportunity for social interaction and group engagement.

5.) Work helps to define a person's social status.

Eventually, the combination of beliefs and actions produce what is known as organizational culture. Such cultures are the composed of various connected, semi-connected, and even conflicting subcultures (Martin &Siehl, 1971). Thus culture is the totality of all the beliefs, symbols, and methods within an organization. When the culture can be adjusted so are the opportunities to subtly influence the course of direction and motivation within an organization.

Implications for Management

Understanding the patterns and methods employees use to make meaning of their environment and the resulting collections of beliefs that constitute organizational culture creates deeper levels of organizational understanding. Through this understanding decision makers can start the process of developing new levels of meaning through language, processes, compensation, procedures, and methods that further benefit both the individual and organization. Through understanding, managers can find mastery over their work environment and encourage higher levels of motivation and beliefs of those under their charge. Focusing closely on the types of behaviors and language management use can further impact the "reality" of employees by modeling appropriate behavior. Furthermore, through training and development the organization can socialize workers into a new way of thinking about their environment and the opportunities to produce meaningful results. To engage effectively in this adjustment to workplace culture will require understanding of a number of concepts.

1.) Employees bring their personal values and beliefs into the organization and mesh them with the corporate culture.

2.) The corporate culture is in flux based upon the thoughts, logic, feelings, patterns, and behaviors manifested to maintain it.

3.) Employees work roles, self-perception, and assumptions are based in their language usage. Adjusting language through more logical symbolism or connections can create additional alignment of worker actions and organizational culture.

4.) Management and employees engage in constant negotiation over the concept of reality (will to power). Management has the ability to adjust employee understandings of their environment.

5.) Training and development employees can lead to new self-concepts, work roles, thoughts and behaviors.

6.) Combining the impact of management language, training, processes, procedures, culture, discipline, and other corporate tools to a few underlining assumptions (corporate principles) can change employee expectations and performance.

7.) Poor and negative attitudes pushed by executives can damage innovation, motivation, and creativity. It creates new realities that have a negative cascading impact on the organization.

8.) Innovation, efficiency and productivity are a direct result of employees understanding of the environment in which they work and their wider understanding of responsibility.

9.) Reality is what society deems it to be…it can deem it to be something else.

Chapter 3
Socialized Self in an Integrating World
Imperium in Imperio!
(An order within an order!)

Socialized Self in an Integrating World

Imperium in Imperio!

(An order within an order!)

It is important to see how concepts of failed openness to the market needs, closed mindedness to other cultures, and false root assumptions can influence the sustainability of an organization. Chapter 2 discussed the concept of reality construction through the use of language, employee meaning-making, and images that present a phenomenon called "quality worlds" that are distinct from others perceptions. These misunderstandings can create conflicts at work, encourage testy labor relations, reduce productivity and cause friction with stakeholders. Understanding how such vantage points and close-mindedness can impact the work environment is beneficial to see how perceptions can limit the growth of the organizations in subtle ways that filter throughout the entire organization. The specific race, religion, or other life assumptions one uses as a vantage point are not as important as understanding hour our past creates our futures. Each person has experiences they use based upon their childhood rearing and intimate beliefs that they used to make meaning out of their environment.

As the world becomes smaller people's mental capacity becomes larger. The development of the human species is adapting to new methods of understanding complexity; thereby creating new systems of thinking, testing and understanding the environment. From groups of a few hundred we have expanded into the millions and once again into the billions. New methods of understanding our place in the world are developing to make sense out of much more complex data. The case presented in this paper is the story of one individual who struggles with her understanding of the environment as she moves from an ethnic community to a global world where she must fulfill responsibilities to others who do not share her understandings. Failing to expand her complexity and increase her order of the mind may lead to resistance by the wider community and failed management approaches that raise costs and reduce productivity. It is important to remember that these concepts are not unique to any particular racial or cultural vantage point but is a universal phenomenon of awareness. The following work discusses Cynthia's developmental stage and how it manifests itself throughout the department in which she has decision-making control. The name Cynthia could be changed with Tom, Sophie, Omar, Pierre, Ivan or any other cultural vantage point. The concepts are universal even though the specific backgrounds may differ.

Cynthia's Background

Cynthia started her career in an entry level position and soon rose in rank and position in her field until achieving an executive position in a short time-frame. She was liked by the majority of employees and those of her ethnic group but appeared to be resented by other executives at the company. Even though she avoided conflict with these other executives she still had difficulty making cross-cultural connections. Cynthia was concerned about being truthful to herself as well as maintaining her position that provided ample power, perks, respect and income. This dilemma continued to grow and create feelings of dissonance between her work roles and her inner self. The higher the responsibility at work the higher the dissonance and frustration she felt. Deep down Cynthia had this feeling that she was misunderstood by others and defined those racial experiences as being subvert discrimination by others.

Cynthia was reared by a family who was fundamentally embedded in and promoters of her ethnic community. Most of her childhood memories were constructed from association with her ethnic identity. Her attendance at church, involvement with local community groups, and education came from a particular vantage point. During her formative years she had few memories or association with others outside her community. This lack of associated understandings of different religions and people created cross-cultural workplace problems for Cynthia.

As a child Cynthia's mother would read to her stories of her heritage, how abuse by others damaged her community, and how proper ethnic girls should behave. Her mother ruled with an iron fist and forced the children down the right path as Cynthia interpreted it. It was the concept of "spare the rod and spoil the child" that gave Cynthia the discipline to be successful. Her whole concept of ethnicity swamped her like a truck trying to traverse deep mud. She was now in a larger world, with higher authority, with multiple competing roles to multiple people with various ethnic and religious backgrounds. Cynthia knew she had a responsibility to treat everyone the same while still holding true to the promotion of her own people who suffered from years of discrimination. This was not something new to her community nor to the rest of the world. She could think of many examples of people with competing interests in their lives. She had no problem with competing interests but did have problems with trying to find a balance.

At work Cynthia was expected to make all types of decisions related to the macro aspects of operations, information systems, labor allocation, management compensation, and her general department. Cynthia made sure that everything worked satisfactorily by being involved in every decision throughout her department. Nothing could be passed, promoted or spent without her approval. She was seen by some as overbearing and to others an example of a successful ethnic woman. Dissent from her management style was often viewed in terms of race embedded issues and these dissenters had a way of performing poorly in their positions. Now facing serious management resistance Cynthia has come to question her own approach to dealing with those who have their own ideas.

Authority and Power is Encased in Language

Michael Foucault, a French philosopher in the 1960's, believed that all human concepts of reality are confined by the use of language (Foucault, 1973). Language itself defines and describes human life. A person's linguistic intelligence and cultural vantage points can create a reality for people with similar language backgrounds.

Applying this concept to a city, state or nation it is possible to see how language may impact cultural vantage points. For example, American English may create a different linguistic understanding of the world when compared to British English. It is the key symbols embedded in our language that help to form our concept of culture (Ortner, 1979). Certainly the people of China and America have different concepts of reality when discussing world politics or economics. The concepts of language create a background of relativism and one's understanding of the world creates a construct of understanding that manifests itself in our beliefs of what is real and not real.

Relativism and constructivism have three underlying assumptions (Freedman & Coombs, 1996):

(1) there is some correspondence between language and reality;

(2) our propositions about our observations are logically coherent; and

(3) there is a reliable and systematic method of testing our observations.

If language and reality are associated, then propositions are based off of observations that appear logical to Cynthia. She will test this logic to create a systematic method of understanding her environment. The way she perceives the world becomes her reality. Cynthia's childhood and socialization process will impact her life and how she approaches life's problems. Nearly all higher order learning occurs through language usage (Halliday, 1993).This understanding and approach filters throughout Cynthia's decision-making logics further confirming or disconfirming that knowledge. Organizations that seek to develop higher levels of innovation and efficiency should understand how language impacts the social realities embedded in organizational culture. It is possible to create a culture through language that manifests itself in compliance, innovation, or performance expectations.

Like most people, Cynthia is using her past experiences to interpret her current surroundings. All new information is interpreted through her assumptions and are based on her past experiences. An action by an employee is seen from a particular vantage point and taken as fact when in reality such understandings are truly subjective by nature. More in focus, the perception of ethnic women in the workplace as strong and controlling may create incongruence on the part of such females who do not personally hold this view (Beauboeuf, 2008). Cynthia is still subject to her childhood beliefs and the beliefs of others that she has adopted as her own through socialization. Yet the subconscious mind is making new connections and understandings that have not yet risen to the conscious level and continue to manifest themselves in anxiety, self-doubt and even more push for environmental control.

Cynthia and Her Operational Decisions

Cynthia has responsibility over the operational decisions of her department as well as the implementation of new technology. Managers who are in charge of these functional areas must come to Cynthia to obtain her permission to implement new strategies and ideas. Sometimes Cynthia tweaks the proposal and other times she requires complete rewrites. One of her favorite sayings is "Being good at being stupid doesn't count". Her impression is that others simply do not do well in knowing how to design and implement long-term strategies. No matter how much she counsels her managers on how to implement new programs, and the direction they should take, the managers do not seem to understand. Cynthia continues to project outward onto others the way she sees and feels about herself.

Constructivism, Performance Measures, and Technology

It is common practice to have performance measures within organizations that help quantify human behavior for organizational evaluation. Performance measures relate to objective indicators of performance that often make their way into perception, compensation, promotion, and power dynamics. Employees often construct their understanding of the work environment from the measures in which they are perceived (Jacobs &Manzi, 2000). Resistance and compliance are associated with how employees understand the value of such measures. Once these concepts are widely adapted as acceptable to multiple members of an organization, a phenomenon called social constructivism occurs (Jacobs &Manzi, 2000).

The methods learned in conducting business within particular occupations can lead to the construction and acceptance of a subjective reality. The use of meanings and interpretations, inherent in occupational approaches, leads to methods of environmental interpretation (Young &Valach, 2004). For example, learning how to conduct analysis in occupational methodologies will impact how a person observes and interprets other phenomenon in their lives. Occupational approaches create a relativity by which the rest of the environment can be tested. This is one of the reasons why psychologists may view the same problem using similar methodologies and come to similar conclusions while those in other fields may interpret the information differently and come to other conclusions. They were taught to accept these methodologies as a way of understanding ideas and concepts.

Even the technology implemented in a business can create social realities for employees. As new technologies emerge, they develop a stream of social action in which people respond to these technological constraints, as well as to each other, to create new constructed realities (Leonardi& Barley, 2010). For example, implementing software that allows for a limited amount of metrics can create new behaviors, thoughts and actions confined by the limits of that technology.

Thus the choice of organizational structure, compensation, expectations, software, etc... that is derived from the decision-making of the individual can cause new social understandings throughout the organizations. When these decisions are self-filtering, or self-enriching, they can cause significant loss of revenue for the investors and a difficult to overturn corporate culture. This is one of the reasons why opening decisions to others can encourage better decisions, higher forms of organizational culture, stronger employee commitment, and in the end higher forms of organizational revenue.

Training can also influence how people perceive themselves and how they act within their work environment. Values can be transferred through training (Altman, 2009). Training can create workplace expectations that are disseminated throughout the organization. When the expectations become ingrained in the workplace values it creates as reality. This reality reinforces social adherence through rewards and punishments.

Organizations, and their managers, can be defined as constructing learning environments that are considered expansive or restrictive (Fuller, et al., 2007). By studying how an organization is designed, how information flows, and who the key decision makers are it is possible to understand how they create new knowledge. Those organizations that suffer from a restrictive environment will have difficulty generating the new knowledge needed to succeed in highly competitive global markets.

Each of Cynthia's decisions focuses more on control than on innovation. She is not able to let managers and employees make decisions on their own because she feels they would counter her beliefs and thus her sense of self-worth. Therefore all programs must be sifted through Cynthia's underlying assumptions that 1.)

she is a successful ethnic woman; 2.) employee populations are like underdeveloped children; and 3.) most people are inherently discriminatory.

Overview of Developmental and Social Constructivism

Cynthia has been struggling with operational issues within her department for a number of years. She has tried to develop teamwork and collaboration but has repeatedly failed in her attempts. The problem is that no matter how much effort she has put forth in encouraging people to work together to generate new ideas she has been unsuccessful in lowering political encampment. People work well alone but cannot work together to solve problems. She feels as though she may have some level of influence in this area but she is not yet conscious of how her behavior impacts others.

Constructivism and reality are identical in the modern world of psychology. A reality is constructed through the understandings we have of the world in which we live. From cradle to grave we continue to take pieces of information from our environment and make meaning of them. This is what some may call "the purpose of life". It is this interpretation of life's experiences that develops our understanding of reality. When the basic understandings of reality are shared among a group we have the underpinnings of a society. This section will discuss the concepts of constructivism, developmental-constructivism and social constructivism as it pertains to reality, development of reality, and the creation of social reality.

Constructivism: Constructivism is our own personal truth, with its individualized logic and reality, that helps us to make an understanding of our environment (Bruner,1986). This understanding is often bipolar using concepts like *right* and *wrong* or *if* and *then* using many different layers of super ordinate and subordinate levels (Kelly, 1969). Constructivism is how we develop meaning from our environment and the actions needed to navigate that environment successfully. For example, if we desire to obtain gainful employment we may construct, based upon our past experiences with the environment, that socializing with the "right people" leads to greater employment opportunities. Others, with different past experiences, may construct that only education and hard work will bring about greater employment opportunities.

Developmental Constructivism: Developmental constructivism is found to exist when individuals make stronger formulated understandings of their environment after psychological states are placed in disequilibrium (Rosen, 1996). It is these environmental challenges that afford opportunities for individuals to develop increasingly complex understandings of their environments. Such new understandings lead to higher levels of sophisticated thinking.

Social Constructivism: Social constructivism ties all human relationships together and makes the argument that individual functioning must be seen in the perspective of communal interaction (Gergen, 1985). Development is viewed in terms of the interaction and information that passes from human to human contact in social settings. It is the collective impressions and transference of this information that creates a social reality.

Cynthia exists within a social reality created from her background as well as from her understanding of the environment. Cynthia's formative years were full of value statements related to how successful ethnic women should act, how they are perceived by society, and the effort they will need to overcome racism. When problems and dissent occurs within her department she often interprets these through her personal filters. The resulting context of her interpretation transfers throughout her department creating an ethnic and authority conscious workforce. The developed social construct encourages others to interpret actions and social relationships within her department through these filters creating additional problems that result in inefficient conflict.

Orders of Consciousness

Dr. Kegan indicates that there are five orders of consciousness that influence our management style (1994). The capacities of consciousness are based upon the complexity of thought as it is derived from the understanding of our environment. As the world becomes increasingly more sophisticated the mind and its ability to understand such an environment must also become more complex. Some may even move so far as to say that as humans are bombarded with data in the *Information Age* and a higher platform of thought must develop if there is hope of keeping the masses productive members of society. Failing to understand the environment in which we live, and the solutions to the challenges we face, could mean constant difficulties in various aspects of life and employment.

As human beings development mentally they take on stronger and more efficient platforms that help them create higher levels of understanding by which to influence their environment. When we transform our thinking we develop,"...*those elements of our knowing or organizing that we can reflect on, handle, look at, be responsible for, relate to each other, take control of, internalize, assimilate, or otherwise operate upon*"(Kega, 1994, pp. 32). It is precisely this ability to understand, change, mold and develop that determines the potential of organizational success.

Even though there are five orders of consciousness this work discusses the third, fourth, and fifth as being part of the highest states of human development. The fifth order is very rare among the general population and is achieved by a select few. Beyond this there may even be a sixth order of understanding a wider global network. Dr. Kegan explains in his book *In Over Our Heads* that these orders manifest themselves in our management styles (Kegan, 1994). Consider the following:

Third Order: The third order of consciousness, as manifested in a management style, embeds the person in the environment. Such a manager needs the direction from others and fails to make tough decisions until it is known what others want. People in such an order of consciousness personalize criticism and project responsibility onto others when the responsibility is theirs. Such managers often have top-down, chain of command type of leadership. They rely on formal positions for power and influence.

Fourth Order: The fourth order of consciousness, as manifested in a management style, allows the person to rise above some of their socialized constraints. Even though such managers collaborate with others they are able to make their own decisions based upon their personal belief systems and thoughts. In other words, they *self-author* their thoughts and beliefs and can find a way to influence their environment. They do not take responsibility for others behaviors or thoughts but will accept ownership for their own. They can rely on formal power structures but are willing to respect the needs of others outside of these formal power dynamics.

Fifth Order: In the fifth order of consciousness a person's identity is not attached to their positional roles or by the expectations of others. They are able to define themselves for themselves. It is through reflection on oneself that they can create higher levels of self-identity. They are willing to work with authority but can also question the nature of that authority. They see themselves in a wider perspective beyond the constraints of rearing, social expectation, and relationship frameworks.

Cynthia can be characterized as existing between the third and fourth order mind or 3 (4). She is aware something is wrong with how she relates to others from different ethnic backgrounds but is having a hard time defining this for herself. As more experience, awareness, and effort brought forth by Cynthia she will slowly move this hazy dissonance into a clearer picture. Once she is able to mentally wrap her arms around the concepts she will begin to deal with and improve upon these relationships. However, the progress from one stage to the next may take years or decades to accomplish. In the meantime she has come to focus her attention on ethnicity and the meaning of that ethnicity through the perspective of others. Only at that point can she claim to be in the fourth order and having power to adapt to environmental problems. In other words, she will have conscious awareness of how her ethnic background is impacting her behavior and will develop strategies to overcome them. Her beliefs and childhood assumptions, as provided to her by her community, have influenced the management style and potential success of the organization. Each technical and social decision impacts the operational aspects of the company and the success of those governed by it.

Such limited understandings of Cynthia can further destroy and damage an organizations potential success. Employees may learn to be dependent on management to make decisions and therefore become less productive and invested in the organization. Decision makers should be aware of these "orders within order" to ensure that their decisions are encouraging and empowering employees to be more innovative (EF), committed (ES), and motivated (ER). They may do this by having an open mind to the possibility that their organization can develop to a higher plane of existence with higher profits and rewards for everyone within the socio-economic group. Encouraging employees to grow and develop within the organization requires a rethinking of the

management style and how it impacts employee understandings.

Conceptual Blending

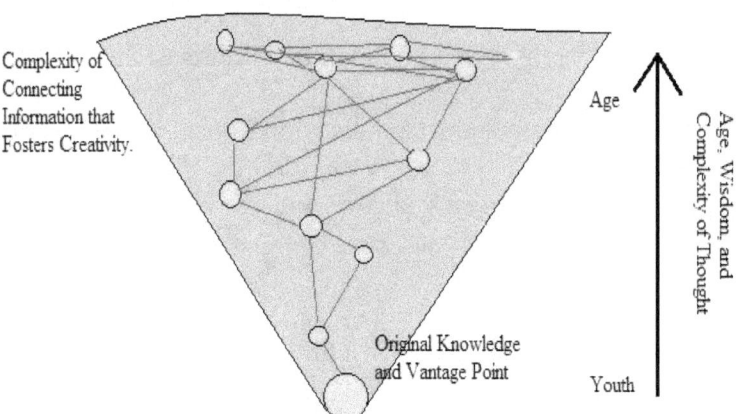

As one becomes more knowledgeable and complex in their thinking they are able to better conceptually blend more pieces of information to create logical rules that apply to more situations. This ability is based upon the schematically ability to connect information in a logical manner and infer rules and root concepts. We start with simple thoughts in the earliest part of lives that become our vantage point.

Chapter 4
Economic Realities
Ut Sementem Feceris Ita Metes!
(As You Sow So Will You Reap!)

Ut Sementem Feceris Ita Metes!

(As You Sow So Will You Reap!)

The Cannibalization of the Young: "*The money changers have taken an unfair share, the politicians enriched their friends, stocks erratically erased generations of wealth, hearth and home turned into revolving credit cards, and the people walk blindly listening to every charlatan and advertisement that flashes before their eyes. They thought that the purchase of just one more product would comfort them like suckling ewes; they will get more thirsty when the teats are dry. Overweight, penniless, unprepared, underemployed, indebted and distrustful they look for some sense of order out of chaos. They do not know that economics is the fishnet of dreams. The world is crashing around them and the next generation is seething with resentment at those who came before. "Where are the crumbs of your promise?" They cling to music, feasts and friends because the generational social contract has been shredded. Their efforts are as scattered as their erratic search for purpose. The parents cannibalized the future of* *the young and the trust is gone! Hope is a homeless vagabond with*

no place to rest."

Today's Economic Reality

The above paragraph is more metaphorical than true but helps to highlight that caring for the next generation, investing in them, and letting them do something important can radicalize them into innovation, efficiency and a brighter future. To save economic health, depleted pension funds, and a declining nation it requires the implementation of principles focused on self-actualization through innovation and efficiency that are rooted in the development of individual's ability to navigate the waters of economic unrest. It is the rearing and enhancement of the American people to new and more complex thinking that creates future opportunities. At present, the national debt has run a tab of $16+ trillion and does not show signs of slowing (Wilson, 2012). The nation needs to set an example by rallying the world markets to invest in a country that pushes for global societal root values and logic.

The economic outlook of the U.S. is weakening as the national deficit increases and employment opportunities appear to be holding with European standards. As the nation attempts to move through the economic difficulties, as a result of increased global integration, it has left a significant proportion of the youth disenfranchised from future opportunities. Public sentiment and faith of the economic system has declined significantly over the past decade. Employers and employees will need to find a path to provide both economic and personal growth opportunities to generations that are swallowed up by a bleak outlook. It is important to accurately view the difficulties of the nation if appropriate solutions are not be brought forward, pondered, evaluated and implemented.

The national trade deficit is rising and leaving many of the youth stranded in their attempts to find economic footing. The U.S. Census Bureau indicates that our current trade deficit is at $559,880,000,0000 (560 billion dollars) per year and indicates the nation has not run a consistent trade surplus since 1970 (U.S. Census Bureau, 2012). The same report indicates that even though service related exports are increasing the increases in product imports far outweigh most of the advantages. Each year the nation falls just a little further behind in its attempt to be internationally competitive and this has huge strategic disadvantages for both the nation and the world.

China's economic strength has been on the rise and has now surpassed the United States as one of the most important trading partners in the world. The U.S. Commerce Department stated that in 2012 China had a $231.1 billion surplus while the U.S. had a $727.9 billion deficit (Forsythe, 2013). This striking figure indicates that the U.S. has limited time to get its economics and political house in order before China will be able to create their own international institutional orders that further its interest at the expense of world's second ranked trading partner. This dynamic shift has been decades in coming and the impact will be more powerfully felt in the decades to come.

Exporting new products and services is important for overall national development. Through providing innovative consumer options the trade deficits decline and the wealth of a nation rises. Such wealth rises through individuals, companies, governmental entities, and investors. Only through year-after-year improvement in national income and governmental management can the national deficit be reduced, reversed, and create a surplus. Without more revenue and efficient government there are few options other than a long drawn out and painful budget cut; or even a more painful economic collapse. What we do today impacts our tomorrow.

Generations and Economic Opportunities as Aspects of Trust

Adding to national revenue problems Generation X (ages 35-44) have further lost confidence in their opportunities to retire with adequate financial resources that last them throughout their old age. According to a Pew Social and Demographic Trends Report,25% of people within this generation who felt they would not have enough money to retire rose to 49% in 2012 (Linn, 2012). Furthermore, data from the U.S. Census Bureau indicates that medium household worth declined from $80,521 in 2005 to $33,200 in 2010. The wealth and savings rate of the American society is depleting at a rapid pace with little hope it will be reversed anytime soon without a well thought out and unified effort to create a comprehensive national plan for growth.

More disturbing is the number of youth that are opting out of the poor work environment. According to Demos in their 2013 report Stuck: Young America's Persistent Job Crisis that 18-24 year old job market participation is behind other generations (Resnikoff, 2013). When compared to other age groups this young and fragile group is backing out of the employment market finding opportunities less plentiful. Furthermore, according to an International Labor Organization report the Global Millennia Generation in developed countries is having a harder time finding jobs than those in Sub-Sahara Africa (International Labor Organization, 2013). Such poor starts in the labor market confines the youth to lower wages throughout their lifetimes. What this and younger groups does and thinks today will influence the success of the country in the future. Changing the economic expectations and engaging assumptions can be beneficial for long-term growth.

Another research study conducted by the Pew Research Center indicates that 61% of households were middle class in the 1970's and then consistently declined to 51% by 2011 ("The Lost Decade", 2012). In the past decade medium income declined 5% but total household wealth declined a whopping 23% showing that the middle class is becoming less financially stable. What is even more shocking is that only 23% believe they are very confident in the future and a large 74% do not believe that working hard will allow Americans to get ahead (comparison between 2011-1999). A total of 85% believe it is harder to get ahead today than it was in the past. More strikingly 62% blame Congress, 54% financial institutions, and 47% corporations. The American public is becoming more aware of economic difficulties associated with poor decision making and may soon find paths to vent their frustration.

Even with economic descent not all the trends are disheartening. A study of over 1,500 people conducted in April of 2012 showed that 33% of people do not trust federal government with nearly 61% indicated a steady level of trust in local government (Pew Research Institute, 2012). At the state level where trust is the highest, people were still concerned that 56% felt money was misspent, division along party lines 53% and inefficient government 51%. Over half of people (54%) believe the federal government is mostly corrupt. The research helps show

how local control and the ability to influence the nature of outcomes fosters greater trust with people.

Even more concerning is a lack of incentives Americans see when deciding to engage, or not engage, the working world and the economy. Without the trust that working hard will produce an equitable reward little effort is likely to be forthcoming. It is an expectancy-value concept. People naturally expect work to produce meaningful results. When this doesn't happen they begin to focus on other areas of their lives. A skeptical youth may simply decide that working hard is not in their best interest fostering a resulting trend of further economic decline. Such youth need an opportunity to learn, develop, and earn appropriate wages from the system if continued effort is to be expected and realized.

The trend of skepticism continues to increase as the nation's financial strength wanes in the face of global competition. According to a Gallop Poll only one in five Americans believe that congress is doing a great job in reducing the deficit (Heavey & Lawder, 2012). Furthermore, a 2013 study by the Pew Research Center indicated that only 28% of Americans trust their government while an increase in trust of state governments have increased 5% from a year prior (Simpson, 2013). This low level of belief in elected leaders creates a distinct question of governmental effectiveness in meeting the needs of its citizenry. In many ways this dissonance may be embedded in the vantage point of key decision makers and their perception of the duties of a public servant. The view of governmental responsibilities must change if there are going to be effective administrative changes by public bodies and organizational administrators.

Governmental, business, banks, and even the media are seen with an increasingly skeptical lens by the public. The 2013 Edelman Trust Barometer surveyed 31,000 people from 26 countries and found that the leadership trust factor was "pathetic" and "leaders are not seen as leading" (McHugh, 2013). The survey highlighted that only 18% trusted the words of business leadership, a small 13% trusting government leadership, and 53% trusting media outlets. In today's world people trust in new avenues of information which include 69% academics and 61% peer groups. The pendulum has shifted away from institutional leaders to information sources from alternative sources.

To add additional salt to current governmental wounds the unemployment rate of youth is expected to increase through 2017. According to the International Labor Organization the global unemployment rate for youth will rise from 12.6% in 2012 to 12.9% in 2017 (D'Monte, 2013). The report moves on to say that even in advanced countries that 35% of the unemployed youth have been out of jobs for over six months. The continued trend damages their enthusiasm, economic assumptions, and skills that will be needed in the future to develop the nation.

Even paying a fair share of taxes can be a detractor from the positive outlook of many people. In January 2013 an IRS watchdog agency Taxpayer Advocate Service, indicated that only 12% of Americans actually felt that entrepreneurs and businesses were paying their fair share of taxes (Temple-West, 2013). Furthermore, tax laws create additional confusion around shared responsibility and require highly educated accountants to decipher. Approximately 90% of taxpayers now need help in filing taxes and over $1 trillion dollars during a financial crisis was wasted in 2011 over improper filings. Despite the advantages offered to tax attorneys and legal agencies the American people are paying the price for this complexity.

Trust and Economic Improvement

Of course this confusion abounds in both government and the population. Inaccurate information, brutal party politics, and excessive special interests have created some false perceptions toward the original root American values. With a possible bleak future, a new way of looking at the nature of business and government becomes important. Developing stronger economic trust with the American people will require proper stewardship and management from the employees at the bottom of the chain all the way up to those who make legislature at the top.

One of the first criteria for constructive change is a positive and accurate self-image. Whether this is a nation or an individual one must face the hard facts of life and adjust their thinking to more constructive outcomes. America is not doing well on the corruption index and ranks 24 out of 150 nations just under Chile (O'Reilly, 2012). More interestingly the study also found that nations with less corruption earned more capital per citizen. Nations that create transparency and ethics within their system are also likely to weather economic difficulties easier than those who do not. Corruption and self-serving government policies are counterproductive to the needs of the nation and the development of its people. It takes a serious toll on national trust which in turn damages economic engagement.

Congress has also been seen in the media as using a vantage point of self-interest in making some of their decisions. Harvard Professor Dennis Thompson states, *"Ethics rules are supposed to make things clear and transparent....They should not require the public or the media to go digging around to make the connections* (Kindy, Fallis, &Higham, 2012)." Some congressional members have been accused of encouraging governmental and legal changes that benefit themselves, family members, or campaign contributors. Self-interest in the governmental creates further inefficiencies that make it difficult for Americans to compete in the global marketplace.

Such self-serving policies damage both a nations present and its future opportunities. Even more concerning is the loss of economic strength and important values associated with principles of democracy. According to the World Economic Forum (WEF) the U.S. is slipping from being the most competitive global economy to number seven on the list ("The World's Best", 2012). The report moves onto state that political battles and growing debt have become major hurdles. Excessive party politics and increased spending have created difficult contractions in society that are causing economic difficulties throughout the entire economic system.

The cost of American debt is beginning to take its devastating toll on the American economy like it has in Greece, Spain, Italy and other places. According to the Congressional Budget Report the national debt held by the public will reach 70% of GNP ("The 2012 Long-Term, 2012). The continuation of such debt is likely unless leaders come together to change how they perceive their responsibilities to the American people and the generations that come after.

As the nation creates complexity in its social structures, the economic system and the belief in its continued growth, is an essential element of social cohesion. Like in Greece, when a nation's financial resources begin to decline social problems rear their ugly head. Each group seeks to find ways of creating advantages and begin the process of developing in and out-group vantage points that further divide the nation. Such cultural and social encampment creates further potentials for clash over economic resources. In many cases these financial strains are manifested in racial, religious, social group and economic arenas. These are areas where people still feel they have influence and accountability due to their closeness.

The 2013 World Development report explains that employment opportunities worldwide impact 1.) standards of living that impact whole concepts of self; 2.) productivity that helps further future growth; and 3.) social cohesion that reduces instability, creates trust, and helps shape values (World Development Report, 2013). Such job creation strategies help tie people to the economic system, create higher self-image, and trust of world governments. The advantages of alignment of basic root principles are important if higher levels of economic activity are going to be developed.

According to Kevin Steinberg, the WEF's CFO, underdeveloped nations rely on cheap labor and resources while highly developed countries rely more on improving technology, worker output, idea development, and coming to innovative solutions. Switzerland is seen as the most competitive country because it has access to more members from the scientific community and intelligentsia. The Swiss also spent more on research and development while improving business-academic relations. Interestingly you will also find that the Internet access in the U.S. is 77.9% while it is 85.2% for the Swiss which helps to push for higher levels of local and global communication to foster new ideas. The development of an educated population helps to set the framework for higher national competitive behavior through the development of more innovative products and services.

Research at Harvard helps to highlight the concept that students overseas are learning at twice the rate as that found in the U.S. (Capus, 2012). Such reports help highlight that an overhaul of the system and priorities is needed in order to maintain a top global position in a world of transformational turmoil. American companies will need highly skilled employees in order to fill orders and develop new solutions to market problems (Capus, 2012). Without a strong focus on the entire educational system there is likely to be great declines of intellectual capital that will be soon followed by economic shifts. What we do today impacts what will impact prosperity 20 years down the road.

Me-conomics makes the theoretical pitch that through the development of employee skill and organizational structural adjustments, self-efficacy can lead to economic improvement on a national scale. This economic improvement will be manifested in new products, greater efficiencies, higher revenues, and greater exports. On a national scale it is through this concept of higher organizational revenue that the economic system can sell more products and services and reduce overall trade deficits. Without a new way of viewing the workplace and the nation there will be little change in the pace of our rapid decline.

It may be even more enlightening to look at the National Intelligence Council's 140 page report from a consensus of 16 intelligence agency findings on trends moving into 2030. The report indicates that megatrends may change the world at an unprecedented rate usurping governments and developing new realities: declining American, European Power, and Japanese global income percentage dropped from 56% to less than half; a population explosion to 8.3 to 7.1 billion people; 60% of world population in urban centers; less food, water, and energy resource; and, more political instability (Gaouette, 2012). This analysis further indicates that American power across the globe is declining and it will need to influence versus control the dynamics. Its power and strength is waning in the face of a rising shift of global power and changing national and international demographics.

The Spinning Economic System

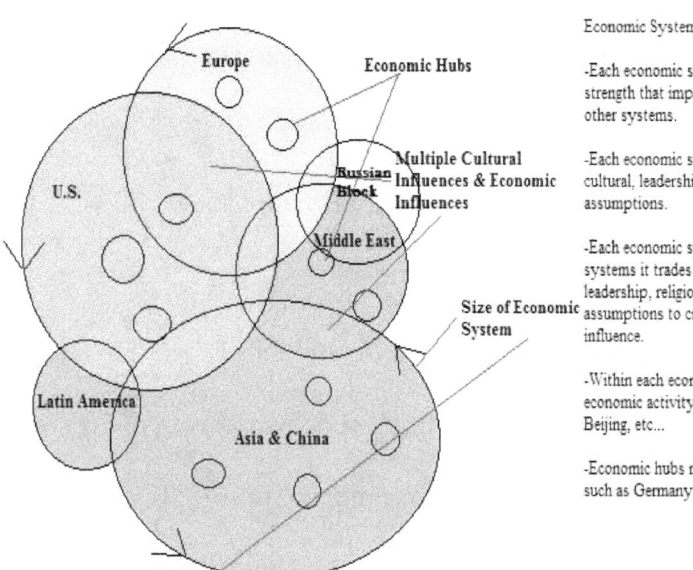

Economic Systems:

-Each economic system has size and strength that impact its ability to influence other systems.

-Each economic system is based upon cultural, leadership, religious, and economic assumptions.

-Each economic system impacts other systems it trades with spreading cultural, leadership, religious, and economic assumptions to create more efficiency and influence.

-Within each economic system are hubs of economic activity (i.e. Detroit, Sun Valley, Beijing, etc...

-Economic hubs may be a country or city such as Germany or Brazil.

The Economic Bloat

Economics is one method of improving the financial and wealth landscape of a nation. Strong nations have the capacity to influence their environments in ways that poor nations cannot. Organizations, decision makers, and investors must believe in their nation if there is hope to continue pushing for higher levels of economic activity and value creation. Corporations make choices to hold onto their wealth, reinvest it in the economy or reinvest in their own operations (Friedman, 2002). The investment choices these organizations make impact everything from the national budget drawn from taxes, financing for schools, development of infrastructure, and even how Americans perceive themselves based upon wealth obtainment opportunities. The value of money moves throughout the financial chains to impact nearly every aspect of social and economic life.

The free market hand is no longer free to act upon the environment due to developments in confused American values not based upon root concepts of liberty and freedom to pursue happiness within the system. A loss of stature means a loss of ability to contribute to social development and adjust the course of events to a more just and practical world. America is sidelining herself due to in-congruent alignment of the system and its values to the needs of world markets. To regain position she must do a little "soul searching" and find those values that are common to everyone. It is a debate about efficiency, innovation, perspective and collaboration.

In 2012 Federal Chairman Ben Bernanke asked economists to stop focusing so finitely on numbers and become philosophers of the future. He comments, "*Aggregate statistics can sometimes mask important information* (Greeley, 2012)." The purpose of economics is not money alone but is the obtainment of goals and purpose. Money is only the scorecard and fuel for the machine. The opportunity to obtain wealth for one's work and ideas creates an environment where economics becomes the fishnet of dreams. At the International Association for Research in Income and Wealth he states, "*We should see better and more direct measurements of economic well being*". It is through the development of proper economic tools and perspectives that we can create higher levels of economic adjustments that put American back on a path to prosperity.

From Ancient Greek generals to modern times people sought methods of seeing and understanding the future for everything from economic activity to military campaigns. According to Alan Greenspan, modern fortunetellers exist in Wall Street in order to analyze what is going to happen in the future (Greenspan, 2007). Economic policymakers seek to use mathematics to understand and make projections about future events. They do so in a method to generate wealth as well as propulsion to society. The more accurately a person can perceive the events that lead to a possible future the more likely they can make appropriate adjustments.

When society is facing difficulties as that seen in a prolonged recession it must make choices that create the most beneficial future results. Me-conomics attempts to create the right economic mix and vantage point to help societal leaders in understanding the long-term benefits of improving employee's global competitiveness. Through pro-worker development policies and proper management techniques the future viability of American organizations and the nation can be improved.

American economic strength has been diluted based upon a host of factors ranging from debt to self-interest. The Great Recession has not been shaken off and has led to economic changes in Europe, the Middle East and the United States. Milton Friedman believes, "*It is a bad system to believers in freedom just because it gives a few men such power without any effective check by the body politic-this is the key political argument against an "independent" central bank*" (Friedman, 2002, pg. 50). It is these checks and balances that exist which allow for an independent governmental body (i.e. central bank) to make movement when it is needed but still be held accountable to the people. Separating the financial money supply and taxpayer expenses too far from accountability mechanisms allows budgets, debt, and political favoritism to expand government spending beyond natural limits, which can have consequences for the American public.

Milton Friedman believes that in the complex-enterprise and money-exchange economy that cooperation should be strictly voluntary under the following criteria (Friedman, 2002): 1.) Enterprises are private and the contracting parties are individuals; and 2.) individuals are free to enter or not enter into voluntary exchanges. These concepts also assume that information being presented is accurate and allows individuals/entities to make proper economic choices. These concepts do not exist in a vacuum and take into account those governmental functions that are necessary to maintain the health of the overall system. As countries move upward in their development they begin to rely less on land wealth and resources and move to new levels of intellectual capital. It is these unmolested intellectual capacities that are key to unlocking America's true economic and social potential.

Milton Friedman further postulates that in the 19th and 20th centuries it is not the promotion of diversity but the creation of common **core values** essential to stability in society (Friedman, 1962). Different economic vantage points and cultural differences that can often separate a nation should focus more closely on the basic principles of American living that apply to all diversified individuals equally. Thus it is important to understand precisely what culturally, religiously, and economically diverse Americans should hold as a similar value system. The integration and acceptance of new cultures and peoples should come with the tying of such peoples to the cultural and economic system of the U.S.

All Should Be Welcome to Engage

Discrimination and bigotry creates inefficiencies in the system by unnecessary separating portions of society from the economic advantages of engagement. Likewise, such surface judgments only create additional errors in judgment that misrepresent the needs of a diverse population that further alienates the entire nation from its destiny. Without encouraging such minorities to engage in the larger economic system they will separate themselves through voluntary and involuntary segregation. Such segregation is against America's most basic principles of truth, equality, and democracy. Creating shared principles requires integration and engagement so that each can stand hand-in-hand in an effort to create a brighter tomorrow for both themselves and their children.

The need for a new way of thinking about society is important for the development of higher societal existence. The process of development has been slowed and reversed over the course of the past thirty years paralleling the decline in economic strength since the 70's. Through mutual self-interest a nation can rise once again. However, before this can happen people must see themselves as responsible and accountable for and to each other. Through development of individual abilities and skills, higher self image and more empathy to work collaboratively throughout our individual efforts can increase economic activity.

Psychopathology, as defined by a lack of empathy for others, has shown remarkable increases over the recent few decades and may cause some of the underpinnings to your problems. According to University of Michigan's Institute for social research measurements of empathy on the Interpersonal Reactivity Index, which includes concepts such as "*I often have tender concerned feelings for people less fortunate than me*," or "*I try and look at everyone's side of a disagreement before making a decision*," has declined 40% since 1979 (Dutton, 2012). Yet it is this empathy and critical thinking that creates the framework for a unified nation that can overcome market challenges. Generally, the more prepared and educated the nation is the more empathy and social development that occurs. It is through the development of ourselves that we can create new ways of approach economic issues from an appropriate vantage point.

Such decline in empathy indicates that society and its leaders have more difficulty in making proper judgments that are beneficial for all people. A lack of empathy will mean more crime, more corruption, party politics, more social unrest and a preying upon the opportunities of the next generation. It is empathy that holds society together by having a shared sense of social behavior and mutual self-interest. When these fundamental premises break down, society also begins to break away from a cohesive group with proper developmental decisions to a more archaic form of existence.

Let us take a look at a young pre-teen boy who decided what reality he was going to live in. He is from the City of Detroit which has suffered decades of corruption and finally fell to its knees under the weight of debt, self-interested decision making and governmental corruption .Joshua Smith decided that he had enough and desired to stand up against the dilapidation of his neighborhood and destruction of his dreams while the majority of adults continued to engage is racial and party politics. His value system hit national airwaves when he presented Mayor Dave Bing a check for $2832.64 to help his devastated city. While the adults were using taxpayer money to promote their political interests at the expense of their people this one boy showed the entrepreneurial spirit and foresight that he has a contribution to make. His reality and self-perception was significantly different from his city's leaders. His mother commented, "*It's not really been about the money...It's been about his spirit being contagious and allowing people to know that we all can do something to change where we are ... It's bigger than just making money for the city. It's about changing **hearts and minds***."(Helms, 2012).

To the youth like Joshua the warning of future financial hardship carries a particular and pungent tone. It is the future of children that will suffer the greatest when the time comes to pay back the debt, suffer collapse, or be left stranded through social unrest. The World Bank's 2013 report seems to echo Joshua's feelings by warning against further stimulus and encouraging nations to focus on education, structural adjustments, governance, and proper conditions that spur investment (Giles, 2013). What legacy are we leaving him? What legacy are we leaving all our children?

There is still hope. Americans appear to be unified on the concept that they want a bright future and opportunities to leave their mark on the global economy. A CBS New York Times poll indicated that 85% of Americans want both parties to, *"compromise some of their positions in order to get things done* ("GOP Delegates", 2012)." They desire "hope" by focusing on basic long-standing American principles that apply to both ideologies. They also want transparency to see that movement has started-to re-authorize the social contract of generational improvement. "A future reality is what we say it is!" A string of thoughts and events that leads to......????You Decide????

The world's business leaders are also coming aboard in support of developing a stronger free market system. In Devos Switzerland the business and financial elite gathered together during January of 2013 to discuss the nature of the financial economy. Even with the finest luxuries of life surrounding them they still feel the power of change and the encroachment of ideas swirling around them like spirits in the mist. Suggestions for improvement include improving the banking system, creating sustainable economies without excessive stimulus packages, and maintaining transparent reforms that encourage higher levels of economic activity (McHugh, 2013). A few have even suggested that reform will need to be seen to its natural conclusion if avoidance of future financial difficulties and social unrest are going to be thwarted.

As the nation faces these difficult and uncertain times we can only be sure about one thing-the need to gain a stronger economic footing together. Me-conomics postulates that by tying all Americans to basic root values associated with positive ethical behavior and pushing for the development of Americans intellectual capacity can this great nation avoid the same fate that collapsed so many predecessors. Through positive action in the development of individual workers and their abilities, can the nation improve upon its global market competitiveness and secure a brighter and more prosperous future. As the debt mounts, economic uncertainty increases, and faith in the system declines, the sands of prosperity slip through the fingers of a people who only wish to feel the bright rays of opportunity. From youth they stood together with a singular saying, *"I pledge allegiance to the Flag of the United States of America, and to the Republic for which it stands, one Nation under God,* ***indivisible, with liberty and justice for all.***"Through the hands and hearts of many can we once again rise to re-authorize the social contract of generational improvement. It is today's thoughts and deeds that create our future. Are we ready to make that choice? We shall all reap tomorrow what we sow today!

Chapter 5
Economic Theories and Market Assumptions
Faber Est Suae Quisque Fortunae!
(Every man is the artisan of his own fortune!)

Economic Theories and Market Assumptions

Faber Est Suae Quisque Fortunae!

(Every man is the artisan of his own fortune!)

So, if you cannot understand that there is something in man which responds to the challenge of this mountain and goes out to meet it, that the struggle is the struggle of life itself upward and forever upward, then you won't see why we go. What we get from this adventure is just sheer joy. And joy is, after all, the end of life. We do not live to eat and make money. We eat and make money to be able to enjoy life. This is what life means and what life is for (Hornbein, 1968, p.21). By George L. Mallory the first man to climb Mount Everest in 1924.

The Economic Approach

Across the world, one can see that economic difficulties abound creating hardships for people and governments. One only needs to look at the riots associated with Greece and the Arab Spring as well as the increase in grass roots protests against the banking industry. Established governmental systems, Internet hacking groups,as well as other important displays of dissatisfaction,show that turmoil is connected deeply to the elements of the economic system. The very decision to move out into the street or into the cyber world in collective action indicates a change in the sentiment of the youth. Employment opportunities and meaningful work influences how people view themselves, their socialization process with others, and how they perceive their stake in society (Akerlof&Kranton, 2010.).Increasing unemployment, lower prospects for the future, erratic global integration and value confusion are creating higher levels of poor self-image within the working population. Ignore the problems of this group and they may become untied to the economic system which has not served younger generations well. It is through economic theory that we can understand how these elements impact the overall function of change and transition.

This potential untying of individual self-interest from that of the nation and the economic system has caused revolution throughout the ages. Understandingthe economics and the principles that hold true are based in individual investment in the system by which people expect to obtain their living and fulfill their goals. Economic activity is a concept associated with trust, which rests in the belief that effort will produce a meaningful reward. When the system fails to offer appropriate rewards it is seen as a hindrance to the population. Such a hindrance isrealized through increasing crime rates, the strangling of small business, the movement of investments overseas, gross national product declines, city-wide corruption, illegal market manipulation, bloated budgets, excessive societal control mechanisms,explosions in public anger, virtual terrorism, and national debt increases. National survival and the enhancement of the next generation rest heavily in their development and fulfillment on a human-to-human level. A reconnection with this population is through the mind in shared vantage points and deeds by providing worthwhile opportunities for economic growth.

The mind is a terrible thing to waste on the whims of a few. The economic system is tied intimately to the trust and perception of its ability to fulfill the needs of its population. Each member who participates in the system through appropriate methods encourages and contributes to its strength. However, a change in value systems can also change the way people perceive governance and the economic tools offered by that system. Much of this understanding is derivedfrom our awareness of the nature of the mind and how it constantly makes meaning from its environment (Damasio, 1994):

1.) The brain and body are seen as an associated organism that includes biochemical and neural regulatory components.

2.) The organism interacts with the environment as both body and mind.

3.) The physiological operations of the mind are a result of the structural-functional ensemble and must be seen in the context of the environment.

It is the person and their physical, mental, and social capabilities that interact with the environment to produce avenues of needs attainment. If an organism learns that the environment has effectively blocked its paths to growth it will rant and rail against that environment. Through encouraging the mind, as well as the cultural and social aspects of community living, higher levels of self-image, individual and societal development can be formed.

Understanding how the individual interacts with their environment helps us understand how decisions are made that lead to economic engagement or disengagement. The environment (i.e. economic system) has a profound impact on all types of decisions people make from the types of occupations they choose, the amount of effort they expend into the system, as well as the products/services where they spend their disposable income.

Economic Mechanics

The growth and development of a nation is an ethical imperative that helps all members of society rise together through mutual trust. Economic expansion in the Capitalistic system is necessary if the future viability of nation is to be secured. Understanding the nuances of national growth rests in part of our understanding of economics. "*Economics, if it is to be a science at all, must be a mathematical science ... mechanics of utility and self-interest*"(Jevons, 1924). The very purpose of economic models is to predict, explain and potentially forecast economic conditions. As a science economics is subject to the same scrutiny of validity, relevance, and significance as other fields of study. Economics is used to explain everything from individual transactions to the cost of national debt. It can even be used to describe how workers make the decision to engage their work environments and contribute to economic development in meaningful ways. Each small component (transaction and decision) impacts the overall success of the larger system (GNP & national debt). They work together by running and influencing each other throughout their operation.

In most economic theories, the individual agent is the central component that makes upthe larger system. An agent is a factor within the process such as a person, business or governmental entity. The economy can be seen as an analysis of how these agents influence each other through evaluations of worth. When the agents continually evaluate each other, they create what is called "the market" where products are sold and economic decisions are made. Economic analysis often focuses on the similarities and patterns of society as they relate to the price of commodities and goods.

The French mathematician Henri Poincaré believed that people do not act alone but constantly watch each other to make decisions (Colander, 2011). This means that each element evaluates his or her environment to make an assessment (i.e.

meaning) of the best choice of action and then apply that action to behavior (i.e. purchase or action) that leads to economic gain. The national economy is derived from hundreds of thousands of people making similar hundreds and thousands of decisions each day by evaluating their environment and putting forth action designed to improve personal gain. Fixing the economic system means understanding these micro components and how they impact the total system and then adjusting processes for improved development and growth.

Meaning making, comparative values, social group dynamics, and economic behavior are associated with this constant comparison and watching of the other market agents. As employees seek to understand their comparative value and worth, they often take notice of comparative wages, work environment, and required effort to achieve goals. Workers are the essential components of the economic system and should understand how their efforts fit within the total system to encourage smoother market adjustments and future national growth.

Economics is often seen in terms of equilibrium in the efficiency of its functioning. *"A characteristic feature that distinguishes economics from other scientific fields is that, for us,*

the equations of equilibrium constitute the center of our discipline.

Other sciences, such as physics or even ecology, put comparatively

more emphasis on the determination of dynamic laws of change"

(Mas-Colell, Whinston& Green, 1995). Equilibrium is viewed as

homeostasis where prices, supply, demand, activity,

unemployment and other factors are accurately measured and on

autopilot without outside influence. This is when the market can

self-regulate and competing forces of the individual agents are in

balance.

Me-conomics is the attempt to create homeostasis in the

system by focusing on the individual elements (socialized

individual) of human production that continually adjusts to global

market changes and therefore improve economic conditions. For

example, through Chaos Theory it has been postulated by Ott,

Grebogi and Yorke that small adjustments in the market can

change the course of a natural economic system without having to

change the fundamental principles(1990). Thus, correctional

adjustments rest not only with organizations but also with the

people who make their livings through these organizations. If these agents are given a chance to grow, develop, learn and change they can adjust with market conditions based upon self-actualization and an accurate perception of their environment.

The vantage point offered is one of micro-adjustments throughout the system from the bottom up versus the top down adjustments that governments are often heavily dependentupon. Through the bottom-up approach the market is more able to make small imperceptible adjustments that accumulate to much larger innovation and efficiency within the total system. Peter Turchin, a Russian-American scientist, believes that throughout time society created elites who implemented more and more rules that eventually suffocate innovation within the marketplace by allowing government to over intrude in people's lives (Ridley, 2010). As government becomes a monopoly it will naturally bring stagnation by trying to pander to groups that attempt to extract more revenue through ever increasing control and expanded governmental budgets. When these decisions filter throughout the economic system, other competing interest beyond individual and societal growth can take precedence; of which only some are beneficial to the entire nation and the welfare of the people.

Economic Welfare

According to the Pareto-optimality Theorem, or commonly called Welfare Theorem, unmolested markets will not only achieve a level of homeostasis but will also create a higher level of moral fabric (Holdsworth, 2011). When a system can run relatively free from market manipulation, whether it is by business monopolies or government, it will eventually produce moral outcomes as it raises people from poverty. This does not make the assumption that government should not have regulatory value over the economy to ensure that the free market is not being molested, but that government should not be in the business of molesting markets. It is the commonality of needs attainment and survival that creates these rules of social interaction and justice through solidifying underlining market premises. These basic root values must apply to any religion, race, socialgroup or positional demographic within a particular society if stable and consistent growth is to be achieved without radical revolutions.

It has been, and will likely always be, governments that derail economic growth and moral imperatives. History is full of societies such as dictatorships, communism, and monarchs that failed to survive because the rules designed to control the populations eventual starved them into either poverty or angered them into revolt. Through time it has been those nations with open markets, open minds, and open opportunities that have done the best against market changes and global competition. It is the free thinking approaches that push people to develop better methods of solving problems that range from individual issues to international issues. Stifling the growth of generations creates a decline in national and international growth.

The Ethical Economic Game

Such markets work best when all of the parts are free to produce, develop, and encourage economic activity. In me-conomics this is the development of the socialization and self-actualization of the worker who at the fundamental components of the system is both the producer and the consumer. The theorists von Neumann and Morgenstern postulated in his work entitled *Theory of Games and Economic Behavior* that economics includes a utility function that is maximized by the patterns of behaviors, probabilities, and maximization of choice (1944). The goal should be to create more rational behaviorsof workers and organizations by developing stronger root value systems based in essential American principlesthat produce higher levels of personal and economic development.

In the book Economics as a *Moral Science* Bernard Hodgson states, "*since the inauguration of systematic studies in economics by the moral philosopher Adam Smith, philosophers and social scientists have engage in an unflagging controversy regarding the proper method of inquiry to adopt in the construction of economic science*" (Hodgson, 2001, pp. 1). To Bernard Hodgson the methodology of Adam Smith was a moral one where economics can foster a higher level of societal moral and economic development. Through the use of proper economic principles people can learn to develop and grow in their endeavors which create better lives for everyone throughout the economic chain.

Working together and enhancing each other is a natural behavior in society; it is not a natural behavior of government. Any party interested in the development of an organization and nations are considered stakeholders who actively seek opportunities in collective action to influence their environment. Organizations are collective groupings where individuals hedge skills and therefore require a level of human development in order to maximize opportunities on a group level. Stakeholder Theory, as postulated by Milton Friedman, indicates that the highest ethical imperative of the members of an organization is to ensure shareholder wealth (Friedman, 1970). Since the development of the theory it has been expanded to include the concept of other stakeholders such as suppliers, vendors, governments, and even society as partial stakeholders to organization development. Each component of society is both connected to each other and makes meaning from each other to understand their environment and overcome economic challenges.

If ethics helps to encourage the development of shareholder wealth, than it is necessary to develop the ethical, social and productive human capacities of employees that has a benefit for the organization, the individual and society. Through Stakeholder theory the firm becomes a resource entity where operational abilities and knowledgecan minimize costs and improve upon market influence (Amit and Schoemaker, 1993). It is the combined abilities and hedging of skills which allow organizations to develop revenue improving efficiencies and innovations (Mohrman et al., 1995). Each organization has an ethical responsibility to foster national growth of itself, society and the nation in order to foster sustainable economic growth.

The Constantly Adjusting System

It can at times be beneficial to see how organizations change to market conditions and the unique contributions employees play in this process. In evolutionary economics, the bounded rationality of organizations changes to meet market challenges. The process of organizational development is one oflearning and adapting whereby entities adjust and develop to problems they are facing (Lall, 2000). Innovation within the economic system can cause levels of uncertainty which might be uncomfortable for many (Schumpeter, 1950). This uncertainty is what helps organizations adjust and change to create stronger future performance. Without a level of uncertainty and discomfort America will not change nor will it have a reason to develop to the next stage in societal existence.

Employees can also be innovative and further the benefits of economic adjustments by solving workplace problems that add up to organizational adjustments which in turn influences the economy. However, if management's function is to control adjustment, or labor unions become obstructionists to change, then the economic system will eventually move further out of homeostasis creating additional misalignment. Like an over spun rubber bandthe system will snap back in place creating major market shifts to correct market inefficiencies and relieve societal pressure. It could result in mass unemployment as people become retrained in new jobs or even financial collapse when expenses are too high to be serviced.

Any time a new market challenge presents itself the economic system naturally begins to adjust. This change can be through organizational adjustments associated with processes and methodologies or at the governmental level when new laws are implemented. What is commonly ignored is the process by which the employees contribute to the overall market and the need for these changes. Employees must also adjust with the system in order to fulfill their own financial needs and personal goals. It is the employees that ensure whether or not an organizational will make that effective transition by adjusting their perspectives and

habits for personal survival and gain. Employees and their
perception have a large contributing factor on the economic
development of both the organization and the nation in general.

The Brain and Economic Decisions

Ultimately employees must make the decision to embrace
or reject the call for change. To this end it is beneficial to see how
the subcomponents of the brain can impact the larger economic
decisions people make. It is through individual choice and
behavior that a personconnects to their work environment or
rejects change all together.In most unmolested cases, where
appropriate information is forthcoming, people will willingly
adjust to new challenges. When management and labor fail to see

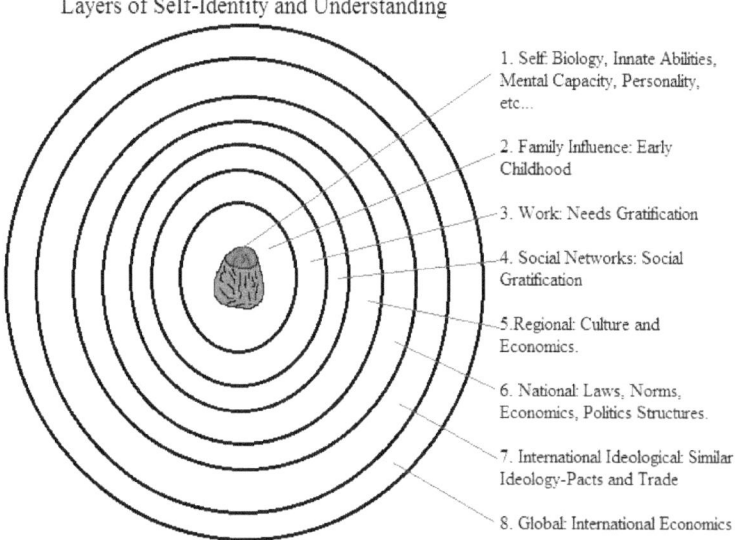

Layers of Self-Identity and Understanding

1. Self: Biology, Innate Abilities, Mental Capacity, Personality, etc...

2. Family Influence: Early Childhood

3. Work: Needs Gratification

4. Social Networks: Social Gratification

5.Regional: Culture and Economics.

6. National: Laws, Norms, Economics, Politics Structures.

7. International Ideological: Similar Ideology-Pacts and Trade

8. Global: International Economics

Our ability to understand starts with our biological skills and abilities that spread out through the integration of knowledge. New information doesn't change previous premises unless we question the nature of that information.

the need for change they may continue to push forward processes and incorrect information that are inefficient and continue to derail appropriate adjustments to the economic system. They maintain the status quo by manipulating the information for selfish ends.It is through accurate information that the individual components of the market (i.e. the brain) find opportunities and choices to determine their behavior.

Inside the crevasses and cracks of your brain are the elemental components to economic activity. Research has helped scientists understand that certain activation centers within the brain lead to economic activities associated with purchasing, ethical behavior, theft, purchases, violate social norms, learning new skills and just about anything else we experience in human life (Ruff ,Ugazio, and Fehr, 2011). A new science entitled neuroeconomics moves to a deep micro analysis that helps to explain the macro-economic system in greater detail.Simply looking at the large economic system as a cold running machine only gives one a static vision; it does not offer an adequate explanation of the depth of human thought that makes up final economic choices. The other vantage point includes the processes within the human brain and how we perceive our personal stake in the larger economic context. Through the internal workings of our heads can begin to see how different choices are made based upon cellular activation that leads to beneficial choices.

The field of neuroeconomics is new and is not yet widely studied at many universities;available information is scarce. This science tries to explain why humans make certain economic decisions by moving deep within the synapses to study neuron-activity. Through this depth and understanding it may someday be possible to see precisely why some people are hardwired to make some decisions over others based upon their paths of neuro-connections. This could further our understanding of how the economic system is made up of these hundreds trillions of economic decisions members of society make each day.

Neuroeconomics takes into consideration the fields of neuroscience, economics, psychology, and computer science to understand how humans engage in decision-making about purchases. The three fundamental questions asked by Neuroeconomics is (Wilson, 1999):

1.) What are the factors computed by the brain and how does this convert to behavior?

2.) How does the neurobiology implement and confine these decisions?

3.) What are the implications for understanding behavior in economic contexts?

The questions attempt to take a look at how the brain functions and controls behaviors when it comes to economic purchases. An attempt is made to study every organ and process in isolation to understand the entity constructed from them (Glimcher, 2004). For example, a person who makes the decision to attend college or pay attention in training versus other worthwhile activities has made a choice based upon their neurological processes. Within the brain, there will be a number of processes and factors weighed before the actual decision to engage or not engage ismade.

Often the choices people make can be studied with an EEG or MRI scan to view what is going on inside their heads. When a person makes a decision between two products the brain will send signals to connect information that ultimately impacts the final choice. The ventromedial prefrontal cortex appears to hold the economic choices and values that subjects use to make a final decision (Wunderlich, Rangel, and O'Doherty, 2010). Every choice workers, managers, and government officials make is processed right inside the front of our heads.

In unbounded economic theories individuals are seen as making rational choices in their behaviors which encourages the economic system to move into homeostasis. Therefore, understanding how people make these choices on a neurological level allows scientists to break down human behavior into smaller components of understanding and analysis. Knowing why some products sell on this level will help us understand why these same products sell on a macro-economic level. It is through these many small choices that a larger system is built.

Understanding why purchases are made does not help us weather the difficulties that we are currently facing as a nation unless new choice opportunities are developed that more appropriately align to individual needs. Burdensome debt loads, excess labor capacity, poor education, poor management, shortsighted decisions, and a weakening economy are going to have an impact on the decisions of this generation and the next. It is important to understand how normal business cycles can become economic disasters when the system moves too far out of homeostasis.

Information and Economic Cycles

Economic cycles are a natural part of life and have occurred in one form or another for centuries. These boom and bust cycles exist in everything from the biological organisms to stock market investing. It is often beneficial to view economic theories on business cycles to understand how imperfect information impacts the national economy as it moves through these growth patterns. Such cycles are many years in the making and can have a devastating impact on the economy if recovery is not forthcoming and systematic improvement not made.

Bob Lucas, a Nobel Prize Laureate, developed a monetary theory of business cycles that helps explain economic growth spurts and decline (1972). To him, inaccurate perceptions of economic factors contribute to these cycles that push the system out of homeostasis. Firms, and their management, only have a limited amount of resources in understanding their environment and typically focus on only that information which is needed for their immediate purposes. It takes a considerable amount of time for firms to figure out what changes in the environment are temporary and what changes are more permanent. It is this inaccuracy that leads to market over action and reaction that veers the system off of course. For example, offering excessive credit with high risk exposure when the economic system is puttering can cause a chain of events that lead to a market crash.

It is advantageous to see how this works in a smaller market. Organizations working within a localized market determine the prices they can reasonably sell their products (Lucas Jr., 1972). Price is impacted by the amount of purchases and the supply of products. With perfect information quantities adjust to supply while prices respond to aggregate spending shocks. Accordingly, with imperfect information firms respond to aggregate spending shocks in the short-run but not the supply quantities in the long run. This can create overproduction which impacts the economic chain throughout a business cycle and even into the next generation.

Just like businesses make improper decisions employees can also make improper decisions. In many ways it is these small decisions that influence organizational decision making and vice versa. These decisions are based upon the available information offered to employees, the organizational pathways to development, and the opportunities presented. Employees are bounded to the organizational rationality and should be encouraged to develop their skills naturally through proper encouragement to create homeostasis with both the organization and market needs. The more accurate and forthcoming the information the more likely they will be able to determine the proper choices and paths to secure their future. Multiple layers of management that block communication influence the overall likelihood that proper environmental understandings will be forthcoming, thereby increasing the quantity of poor decisions.

With proper information and trust in management a generational contract is born. A model developed by Paul Samuelson (1958) helps to further explain the concept of a generational contract. Two generations, one young and one old, are engaged in the market. The young sell part of their production to the old who give the young financial compensation. The young hope to save some of the money in the anticipation of purchasing products from the next generation. The entire process works off of anticipation and an implied social contract. It is believed that by producing today the young will reap the rewards of their work tomorrow. Risk makes its way into the system when short-term decisions based upon an individual, a group, or a generation seeking advantage over the next generation and forget that tomorrow will someday come.

The wider impact of this veering off of course can impact generational growth potentially breaking the generational economic growth cycle. Artificially adjusting the market in one generation could have an impact on the economic viability of the next and so on down the time-continuum chain. Using the above example it is possible to see how an economic problem is created if one generation cannot produce and save in order to purchase from the next generation. As the money supply dries up, underutilized human capital, and contraction limits employment opportunities it will effectively leave one generation worse off than preceding generations. To fix this problem may lay in expanding the market to other nations (i.e. selling of products and services) to use excess labor capital, improve investment returns, and create natural liquidity in cash flow.

According to Dobrescu and Paicu (2012), when additional monies are injected into the system the prices of products increases which causes inflationary pressure. In essence, the products are rising in monetary terms but not in their real earthly value. An injection of money from a large generation of people with easy credit will impact the amount of money available for the next and smaller generation who are selling their production. A large market expansion could cause a comparatively large contraction later. The use of credit and debt without regard to true factors of risk and reward will artificially inflate the system while ignoring underlining market principles. A contraction in such a situation is likely to be more devastating when products "real worth" becomes realized (i.e. housing crisis).

We learn that as economic firms overact to market increases they will increase production based upon price increases. If credit markets are artificially expanded to increase purchases it hedges out the next generation's purchasing power and money supply. One of the generations will need to pay the debt back. There will be a large contraction, or market flux, when this money is not available for purchases of products that keep the generational exchange of money and labor in full growth. As the market contracts the GNP and economic system slows down. The cost of debt becomes over-burdensome in an economic recession creating additional difficulties in market clearance.

Boom and bust cycles are common in un-manipulated economies but become radical pendulum swings in manipulated markets. Such boom and bust cycles often follow an increase in production and then a quick contraction as resources are used up (Sherman & Hunt, 2008). The same cycle can occur in credit markets, production of goods, housing prices, or even entire economies. When boom and bust cycles are large it can impact generational growth patterns as seen in the economic recession. Before an economic system can move back into homeostasis it must complete a market clearing of excess supply and demand. However, long periods of clearing may change the underlining assumptions of the entire economic system. Once the assumptions are changed societal shifts and resistance erupt. These are the times when the world changes and throws out inefficient market structures.

If decisional processes impact choices consumers make it also influences the choices employees make as well. Employees that seek to gain advantages within the workplace will make choices throughout their employment careers. These choices could be based in self-development, particular paths of employment, or the types of rewards they are willing to expend energy on. Through the development of rational decision making within organizations, employees will be more able to make logical choices as it relates to their economic opportunities. In such a situation the market assumptions have not been altered.

Through understanding economic evaluations we can see that each theory rests on a level of homeostasis within the market. This homeostasis is developed when individual contributors to the economic system continually adjust to changes in the market. Developing employees through appropriate management techniques furthers the economic system by helping them adjust and make proper efforts in doing so. It furthers the market assumptions by sending the message that production will result in

personal growth. Encouraging employees to be innovative,
satisfied, and motivated will help them create higher levels of
achievement that contribute to the overall attainment of this
homeostasis.

Keynesian economic theory has been under increased
scrutiny as the U.S. national debt load increases and the economy
suffers from a long period of recession. The theoretical standpoint
of the Keynesian model is one of a mixed bag where those
elements that would have a positive impact are often drowned out
by inefficient governmental waste, political favoritism, and the
cost of servicing the debt. Under certain circumstances the policies
can help stave off economic collapse but fail to bring about
positive benefits the longer it is used. It suffers under the law of
diminished returns.

According to the U.S. Census Bureau an era between
1790's to 1930's only saw deficits in government spending in
approximately 38 years. Most of this debt was short-term and a
direct result of increased costs of war or economic downturns (Lee,
2012). Total federal budgets ran at approximately 3.2% of GNP
when compared to nearly 70% of GNP today (The 2012 Long-

Term, 2012). At such a high debt-to-earnings scenario the Keynesian approach loses its power to encourage future economic benefits. It is more beneficial to spend any resources on the development of the individual within his working context and skills to create long-term returns on investments. Education is a central aspect of future growth as the nation tries to maintain intellectual and economic advantages over other nations.

Chapter 5 Summary

We know that the economic system is made up of individual elements. These elements are often seen in terms of an individual's economic choices based upon their understanding of themselves in context to family, work, social group, regional hub, nation, and international economic environments. However, the human being is the essential element whose micro decisions impact the viability of the entire country over time. They make their decisions based upon understandings found in their social networks work environments. These decisions are based in how they perceive themselves in the world around them. Using both the bounded rationality of organizations and unbounded rationality of individuals, innovative adjustments can be made that encourage more exact levels of economic homeostasis. It is through the development of the individual's ability, through the me-conomic vantage point of socialization to root values, do they have the ability to be innovative, satisfied in their work assignments, and motivated to pursue goals that both the ethical imperatives of organizational and national stakeholders can be realized. Yet if the underlining assumptions of the market change due to excessive recession then the societal contract breaks and social resistance becomes more common. As the nation seeks to develop methodologies to regain its economic footing, it will need to seek the creation of higher levels of ethical standards that apply to all individuals in order to create systematic justice and greater levels of trust among the next generation. Failure to make changes now, through our understanding of our world environment, will mean a less competitive future with possible economic collapse and radical market resistance by a generation who may no longer view the relation between effort and reward as progressive under established market assumptions.

Chapter 6
Me-conomics Formula: Adjusting Reality in a Socialized Workplace
Ex Cultu Robur!
(From Culture Comes Strength!)

Ex Cultu Robur!

(From Culture Comes Strength!)

$$\sum \left[\left(\frac{\sum\limits_{1=i}^{n} EF_1}{N_1} \right) + \left(\frac{\sum\limits_{1=i}^{n} ES_1}{N_2} \right) + \left(\frac{\sum\limits_{1=i}^{n} ER_1}{N_3} \right) \right] \over 3$$

The Me-conomic formula rests on three main factors that include employee innovation, motivation and satisfaction. Each factor was been chosen for its ability to create sustainable benefits for organizations on multiple fronts in an effort to increase revenue and positive affectivity of employees. Through the development of the individual an organization can create higher profit margins and benefit society through the greater development of human capital. It is through this human capital that higher levels of economic activity can create new ideas and generate additional revenue for both organizations and a nation. This is the time where greater managers must become great leaders in order to spur investment opportunities and higher levels of national influence. Each organization makes the choice to engage in employee development or continue down the path of improper demoralization and control structures that leave little reason for employees to engage their economic environment. Through the American entrepreneurial spirit there comes strength through culture. It is up to organizations to foster this spirit by creating environments where workers can develop, innovate, and overcome.

As the nation seeks methods of regenerating itself into a new paradigm of global competition it will need new ideas to create additional products, services, and operational methods. During the economic downturn many leaders have focused solely on cutting costs and reducing waste within their operations. They have taken a denominator approach. Even though these processes work in the short run they do not address adequately the need to create more revenue by solving consumer needs on a global scale. The new era of American development will harness the unique cultural strengths of the American spirit and innovative spirit. Through the development of employee's minds does a new path open for higher levels of efficiency and development to regain lost hope and a brighter economic outlook.

Employees have innate instincts and desire to be valued for their intellectual, social and physical contributions. The formula helps employers find a methodology for inclusive management techniques that improve upon organizational capabilities by fostering these instinctual desires to succeed and develop. Through enhancement of employee's abilities the organization can further capitalize on new revenue streams that create higher levels of global competitiveness. Applied on a national scale and the possibilities are only limited by the capabilities of the human mind and its ability to overcome challenges.

The concept of motivation entails the instinctual desire to achieve one's objectives in both personal and professional arenas. Employees who are motivated produce more at work and are able to contribute more to the financial successes of the organization are an invaluable asset. If employees can find need fulfillment within the workplace this influences other two factors of satisfaction and innovation. The accomplishment of goals creates a perspective of social and financial values within their work and social groups.

Innovation is a process of problem solving that helps organizations provide customer orientated products that have market appeal. As employees continue to solve problems they encourage more efficient operations and reduce waste through their collective input. Furthermore, such innovation is the directed volition of motivation that can be a method to obtain higher levels of personal and social recognition. It is this problem solving and social recognition that fosters ever higher levels of motivating effort and additional opportunities for organizations to increase revenue streams.

Employee satisfaction describes the positive affectivity employees feel toward their work environment and social group. Organizations are socio-cultural groups that have values, norms and beliefs. If employees feel connected to their workplace and the people they work with they will cause less resistant labor problems and therefore reduce expenses related to turnover, medical costs, absenteeism, poor production, and social problems. Satisfaction also impacts employees' desires to put forward effort as well as solve organizational problems which can influence the success of the entire organization.

Even though the three factors are associated and impact each other they are not the same mental constructs. Each factor impacts the other factors and enhances them but maintains their own identity. As one factor increases it will also be an indication of and an influence on the other two factors. Me-conomics is the process of socializing workers using these three factors as a gauge, to new and more productive habits and behaviors that enhance both themselves and the organization. Below you will find additional descriptions of how these factors are associated. In the follow chapters each of these factors will be discussed in greater depth.

The Factors of Satisfaction and Motivation

Employee satisfaction and reward are associated concepts that work together to create a more competitive work environment. According to Radovanovic & Savic, "*Today is the time of knowledge, creativity innovation and information*" (2012). The research helps highlight how motivation and satisfaction are connected in the minds of workers even though they are two different concepts. Despite this difference they have some connecting traits focused primarily around the environment and the activities of managers.

A study conducted at a number of companies used employee survey questions that help highlight what encourages employees to be motivated and satisfied.

1.) What is the work climate in your company and how does it influence your motivation and satisfaction at work?

a) positive and stimulative for work and satisfaction 80%.
b) negative and not stimulative for development and satisfaction 20 %.

2.) What are the most frequent present factors of motivation and satisfaction for work in your company?

a) monetary compensation, 56%
b) the nature of the job 30%
c) career development 20%

3.) How much does praise affect motivation of employees for work and for their further development?

a) a lot 70%
b) a little 20%
c) not at all 10%

4.) Does the pronounced sanction for employee inactivity influence

the performance in further work:

a) It does not, 70%.
b) It should, 20%
c) It does, 10%

5.) Is it necessary to establish work performance evaluation, as

stimulating factor for work and development (occasionally, all the

time):

a) Yes, 65%
b) No, 25%
c) Maybe, 10%

6.) How much is the company management obliged to deal with

the issue of motivation of employees and their satisfaction?

a) Yes 95%
b) No 5%

7.) How much is the motivation of employees in your company

influenced by: individual characteristics, job characteristics, and

characteristics of the company?

a) individual characteristics, 40%
b) job characteristics, 30%
c) characteristics of the company, 30%

8.) How much is satisfaction of your employees influenced by

reward, work atmosphere, colleagues at work and the job itself?

a) Reward 40 %
b) Work atmosphere 20 %
c) Colleagues at work 20 %
d) Job Itself 20%

The survey finds that the environment and how managers

engage workers is a large factor in creating motivation and

satisfaction. Furthermore, the use of discipline doesn't detract from

this environment. In such situations when employees are not

meeting minimum qualifications for the job nor are they

complying with important business rules discipline doesn't detract

from their experiences as long as management is focused on

engagement and development with the employee. The removal of

employees that fail to contribute to the success of their

organization, themselves, or their social group is a justifiable

action that may lead them to develop somewhere else and at some

other time.

Despite the potential complaints by employees they instinctively know when they have failed to meet some important criteria. Taking the time to explain how rules help the individual, their fellow workers, and the organization further solidifies this tacit and implicit knowledge. The more managers can frame improvement and discipline in a pro-employee developmental perspective the less damage to cultural morale while greater the opportunities for further satisfaction.

The researchers also suggest that strong human resource functions are important in enhancing this creative environment. Employees adopt motivational systems through their perceptions and personal opinions from a stable system of beliefs that predispose them to behave in a certain manner. The more tied the employee is to the organization the more likely they will be able to accept these organizational premises and adapt them as their own beliefs. The responsibility of human resources leaders is to track and gauge not only human capital but the cultural environment of the workplace.

The Association of Motivation and Innovation

The nature of work and the organization is changing. As this work becomes dynamic, uncertain, knowledge orientated, and ever adjusting it will rely more heavily on creative ideas of employees (George, 2007). Intrinsic motivation and innovation have important associations that should not be overlooked by organizational researchers. It is through this internal motivation that new ideas and concepts become born through associating and connecting new information in unique ways to solve larger problems.

Intrinsic motivation refers to the desire to expend effort based upon one's interests and enjoyment of the tasks being performed (Ryan & Deci, 2000). It is an internal desire for self-fulfillment, development, and accomplishment outside of the realm of extrinsic rewards. In history it was the desire of these intrinsically motivated and creative individuals that changed the nature of industry, methodology and even patterns of life by bringing forward ground breaking ideas and concepts.

Compensation was a beneficial solidifier of motivation but not the main purpose for the development of great ideas and outcomes.

Intrinsic motivation is believed to enhance creativity through positive affect, cognitive flexibility, persistence, and risk taking (Shalley, Zhou, & Oldham, 2004). Each of these concepts are necessary in order to guide an intrinsically motivated person to higher levels of idea generation, analysis, and eventual solution. Motivated Information Processing Theory indicates that motivations shape the cognitive processes, the selective information they are aware of, how they encode information, what information they will remember in order to solve novel problems (Kunda, 190).

Through cognitive flexibility employees are able to engage in pro-social behavior that encourages the development of new ideas. When employees take the perspective of the "other" they are more likely to develop useful solutions to a wider group of people (Mohrman, Gibson, & Mohram, 2001). It is this pro-social behavior which encourages them to solve problems in ways that appeal to others (De Drue, Weingart, & Kwon, 2000). Through the perception and perspective of solving problems through customers, managers, employees, and shareholders vantage points can a person find solutions that fulfill the needs of and satisfy the desires of larger groups creating higher levels of creative utility.

There are a number of criteria for motivation to be successful in creating innovation. Positive affectivity stimulates creativity by broadening the range of cognitive information, expanding the scope of attention for obtaining information and ideas, and creating flexibility for identifying patterns and association between complex ideas (Amabil, Barsade, Mueller & Straw, 2005). It is the ability to move out to wider concepts and environmental facts that allow a person to reconnect information in new ways to solve complex problems. In order for this to happen one must display an "open mindedness" to new thoughts and ways of perceiving the environment.

Innovation and internal satisfaction mix with self-confidence to maintain task persistence. Through Self-Determination Theory it is the fostering of confidence and interest that intrinsic motivation encourages employees to maintain effort on challenging, complex and unfamiliar tasks (Gagne & Deci, 2005). Moving into the "unknown" is not easy for many employees and can be quickly discouraged by poor managers. Without a belief in one's abilities there will be a lack of confidence that such activities will bear fruit or have a positive outcome.

The beauty of internal motivation is that when it develops into a pro-social context it expands its potential solutions to have the largest possible impact. Psychological research has shown that such pro-social behavior in internally motivated and creative individuals push for solutions that impact multiple-generations (McAdams & de St. Aubin, 1992). The wider the impact the more problems its solves for people and the more financial and social worth it is to the organization and nation.

According to a study of military personnel, water department employees, and in-house laboratory manipulation, conducted by Grant and Berry, it was found that high intrinsic motivation with pro-social behavior created higher levels of creativity, perspective taking, perceived choice, task interest and pro-social behavior than any other combination levels of high/low intrinsic motivation with high/low levels of pro-social behavior (2011). The main findings of the study indicate that intrinsic motivation is more successful in developing creativity when individuals are socially motivated to take the perspective of others and use innovation to solve problems.

Through the motivation, innovation is developed. It has important social underpinnings associated with employee satisfaction and social group dynamics. As employees master skills, gain new information about their environment, and explore the wider social context of their work they use their higher levels of motivation and self-efficacy to complete complex and unfamiliar tasks. It is through the encouragement of innovation, employee satisfaction, and motivation that organizations can further the development of new lines of revenue and financial success.

The Connection of Motivation, Innovation, Satisfaction

Interesting research entitled *Social Capital in Human Service/Child Welfare Organizations: Implications for Work*

Motivation, Job Satisfaction, Innovation, and Quality by Salvador Montana helps shed light on how Social Capital Theory explains organizational performance through the factors of innovation, satisfaction, motivation and quality. Such research is limited in its causality and accurate terms of measurement but does create higher levels of understanding that focuses on defining how group values can generate higher levels of performance.

Four thousand and six participant (4006) surveys were retrieved from human service industry workers in Texas. The age of participants varied and the education level of the workers ranged from high school to graduate degrees. The work environment was considered bureaucratic with clear lines of authority and top-to-bottom styles of management. The environment did not appear to offer clear opportunities for employee based environmental improvement.

"*The purpose of this study is to explore ways public human service organization can improve the provision of services they provide to the public* (Montana, 2006, pg. 7)." The study creates a backdrop explanation of how even in large governmental organizations there is the possibility of improving the services offered through proper socialization efforts. Furthermore, it lends credibility to the factors of innovation, motivation and satisfaction as having significant influence on performance improvement as postulated by Me-conomics (the socialized self within an economic system).

According to the theoretical model proposed by the researcher there are four dimensions of social capital:

Social Capital

1.) Structural Dimension: Network Ties, Network Configuration, Appropriable Organization

2.) Rational Dimension: Trust, Norms, Values, Identification

3.) Cognitive Dimension: Shared language, codes and narratives.

4.) Social Knowledge: Exchange and Recombination, Explicit and Implicit Knowledge.

Each of these dimensions is theorized to lead to innovation, satisfaction, motivation, and quality. The eventual result of these four factors would theoretically result in improved organizational performance within the bureaucratic human service industry. The study attempted to see if these four characteristics lent support to the model. The study did not seek to find causality between the characteristics but instead attempted to find significant associations.

The results of the study indicated that there was a strong correlation between normative factors linked to social capital which include information, knowledge, networks, trust, goal setting, group cohesion and coordination toward group goals. These social and normative factors had influence on innovation and satisfaction to a stronger degree and a weaker association with motivation and quality. The weakest association was with quality leaving this as a possible extra variable without strong influence and a minimal connection to the other three.

The researcher concludes that findings of the multiple regression analysis indicated that social capital has the greatest predictive strength on innovation, motivation and satisfaction. In essence when the culture and conditions of the organization are set to the right tone an organization can improve upon these three variables. It is the social group that reinforces these expectations and behaviors and leads to higher levels of performance. It is through this socialized and organizational learning process that companies can enhance overall performance even in bureaucratic institutions such as child welfare organizations.

The author contends that even though Social Capital Theory has been around for some time it has limited research because it is strongly conceptual and abstract without strong ability to measure multiple factors for correlation. Minimal research has been associated with larger populations but not strongly focused within the organization. Valid measures have been difficult to find and that such concepts will need to be conducted over a larger spread of time through multiple researchers. The author further indicates that the highly conceptual nature of the variables will need to be better defined before significant measurements can be taken to improve organizational performance through such a lens.

The research also indicates that innovation, satisfaction, and motivation are measurements of a deeper need for humans to develop and grow within their organizations. Such constructs are manifestations of a need to achieve in one's life. This achievement is embedded in the very nature of human life and the culture by which it manifests. It is up to managers and organizations to find the path to tap the potential of the human mind to create higher achievement on an uncharted destiny.

Innate Human Desire to Succeed

The innate nature of man is to contribute to the development of the organization and society. Through the purposeful enhancement of individual workers, society can reap the rewards of higher levels of performance. Such performance is a natural instinct of man when given appropriate guidance and opportunities for development. Managers can contribute to the economic development of their society by fostering the instinctual self-interest of individuals to contribute to survival of the entire organization.

"Chief among those instinctive dispositions that conduce directly to the material well-being of the race, and therefore to its biological success, is perhaps the instinctive bias here spoken of as the sense of workmanship." -Thorstein Veblen

Instincts have a large impact on why man engages in meaningful work. As a biological creature he seeks to develop the well-being of his race and in essence his own overall success. Within the context of the organization, instincts are tied to behavior and eventually to the methods by which people find needs attainment. Instincts seek concrete objects while habits are the methodology of achieving these concrete objects (Brette 2003).

In the literary work Instinct of Workmanship Thorstein Veblen discusses man and his instincts as the elemental parts of an economic system. To him man, through his natural development, is instinctively pushing himself to learn, innovate and create more efficient methods of ensuring survival (Veblen, 1914). The development of tools and machines is a natural part of this process (Ayres 1958).

Understanding human behavior is important for understanding both organizational development and economics. All socio-economic development theories rely on human behavior as their foundational understanding (Jensen 1987). Therefore, psychology and economic development within an organization, or a nation, are inherently tied to behavior that can be adjusted through development of new habits based in instinctual expression. These concepts are spawned by Darwinian explanations of biological development and adaptation.

As innovations improve they naturally create structural changes in the environment. The structural changes further adjust people's thoughts and habits that eventually lead to alignment with organizational and societal needs. The process of adjustment and adaptation continues because it is within man's best interest to survive, develop, and overcome the challenges in his environment. It makes little difference if they are natural or manmade structures. The creation of institutions and their development fits within this instinctual pattern of survival.

"The typical human endowment of instincts, as well as the typical make-up of the race in the physical respect, has according to this current view been transmitted intact from the beginning of humanity. . . . On the other hand the habitual elements of human life change unremittingly and cumulatively, resulting in a continued proliferous growth of institutions. Changes in the institutional structure are continually taking place in response to the altered discipline of life under changing cultural conditions, but human nature remains specifically the same. (1914, 18)"

Society develops by creating ever higher levels of efficiency with its use of tools and effort. Therefore, as society develops and becomes more complex man creates the need for division of labor and institutional development in order to foster higher levels of utility (Edgell 1975). With such an understanding it is possible to see how successful organizations are more able to capitalize on of the instincts inherent in every person's need for survival.

Let us put this within an example. People are naturally driven by their survival instincts to develop and innovate.

Employees use the tools available to them, through the job specialization they have learned, in order to create the most efficient use of their time. The more skill they have, the less time they spend to fulfill their financial needs. Managers not only control this function within an organization but also have a responsibility to encourage workplace adaptations that benefit the organizations. Empowering employees to use their natural instincts to create habits which find solutions to personal problems can also be used to find solutions to organizational problems.

Employee Empowerment

Empowering employees is more than offering a few trinkets of appreciation and turning a backside to the fundamental principles of human needs. Improving employee empowerment requires consistent positive affect of behavior that builds trust and commitment to organizational expectations. Through proper management techniques employee empowerment can lead to a higher functioning organization that not only saves costs but better hedges human abilities.

Empowering employees has a number of benefits for companies that seek to make improvements within their organizational approaches. Employee empowerment has been seen as a way to increase motivation, morale, satisfaction, commitment and innovation (Ford & Fottler, 1995). These elements work together to create a stronger organizational approach to employee management. Employees who feel they have influence over their environments are much more likely to feel ownership over it.

According to Thomas and Velthouse (1990) empowerment is associated with intrinsic task motivation. Such task motivation reflects four cognitive approaches which include meaning, competence, choice and impact. Through positive affect in these areas employees are able to create higher levels of positive orientation and empowerment.

Meaning: The work should have meaning to the employee and the organization.

Competence: The employee should feel as though they are gaining mastery over their work.

Choice: The employee should feel their line of employment and their work tasks are of interest to them and a personal choice.

Impact: The employee should feel their work is making a difference.

Importantly, empowerment requires a level of organizational fairness. The perceptions of fairness are influenced by the equity of reward distribution and interpersonal respect (Lind & Tyler, 1998). Employees, who view the reward process as unfair and who are not treated equitably will not be empowered to work harder, solve problems or engage the organization. They will keep quit and let others make decisions. They will become passive contributors to the environment.

The concept of fairness can often be perceptual by nature. Such perceptions abound when employees feel that they have not been treated with ethical appropriateness associated with common understandings of civility and dignity (Greenberg, 1990). It is these socialized understandings that contribute greatly to the level of willingness to be proactive within the workplace. Fairness affords the opportunity for employees to understand their environment and then display mastery over that environment. Organizations that have chaotic approaches to management will lower employees' ability to understand their environment and put effort forward. Consistency and small adjustments that are fully integrated are important for overall success.

Despite these benefits there are a number of barriers that impact the success of employee empowerment approaches. These barriers are often related to the trust and fear between management and labor (Andrews, 1994). Without strong work relations and social equity there is a lack of trust that management will follow through with expectations and fear associated with management styles that impact the feelings of fairness among employees.

Even small negative events can add up overtime to reduce empowerment (Abelson, 1985). Employees who have been treated unfairly, inappropriately, or have witnessed failures of management will accumulate such instances to make an impression of their work environment. Encouraging these detractors from empowerment within the workplace over time can even create a culture lacking of empowerment that impacts the financial abilities of the organization. They begin to conceptually blend these concepts to create a methodology and pattern to approaching problems.

Detractors are not just one-off instances of unfair treatment. Such actions drain motivational energy which further creates ineffectiveness in managerial effectiveness and innovation within their departments (Spreitzer, 1995). The longer such detractors exist the more ineffective the manager will become in his/her approaches. On an organizational scale this can have large financial consequences as the employees mentally separate themselves from their managers.

Through trust organizations can improve labor management relationships and overall organizational effectiveness. Trust impacts the overall outcome of individual cooperation and group cohesiveness (Alexander & Ruderman, 1987). It is through this group cohesiveness with shared senses of behavior, purpose and understanding that a positive organizational culture can be built.

Empowerment is not a workplace concept that can be implemented and pulled at the whim of executives. It must be fostered throughout the organization, management techniques, and organization culture. Those managers who detract from an empowerment strategy should be removed and replaced by those who can realize higher levels of worker performance as well as organizational development.

Explanation of Factors and Formula

In the Me-conomic formula each factor EF, EM, and ES can have multiple sub-factors that generate a composite score. For example, an organization could provide strong training, idea generation processes, and employee involvement but not have a strong grasp of information sharing pathways. This wouldn't mean that the organization doesn't have the potential to be innovative it indicates that the strength of this function should be improved if it fits within the strategic approach of the organization. Some organizations may focus on a certain collection of factors that fit within their strategic approach and market environment. Each of the three factors in the formula may have 10-30 different perceptual sub-factors that make up the score in the category. Future research may add additional relevant components that can be measured, incorporated and hedged within the formula.

It should be pointed out that there are two beneficial methods in measuring these factors. One method is to use an employee survey while the other is to research operational data to discover areas of weakness. Employee awareness and perception create a reality within the workplace by which employees understand their world and its available options. Perception of employees is their reality when they make decisions to engage the organization. However, perception can often be followed up by marked improvements within the sub-factor by making important changes within the operational function of the organization. Once weaknesses have been discovered the actual improvement in these operational constructs would require research and adjustment as to finding the most beneficial and cost effective improvements.

The formula is considered floating in the sense that as additional factors are found in future research they can be incorporated within the categories to create ever more legitimate measurements. The formula is used as a perceptual understanding of how employees perceive their environment and possible methods of improving this perception. Where there is weakness there is also an opportunity to make structural adjustments that improve the organization. It should be remembered that this is a formula from the employee/managers perspective and can be used for organizational/operational adjustments in policies and procedures. It is not an exhaustive list of all perceptual possibilities that could be included at a future date.

Series of Factors

EF: Innovation Series

-EF (Innovation Series): The innovation series relates to both the potential and actualized abilities in developing solutions to problems. Through the ability to use knowledge in new ways organizations can create stronger market presence.

ES: Satisfaction Series

$$\left(\frac{\sum_{1=i}^{n} ES_1}{N_2} \right)$$

-ES (Satisfaction Series): The satisfaction series indicates the satisfaction and enjoyment workers feel when working for the organization. It takes into account group relations. The more satisfaction employees feel the less disciplinary problems and turnover an organization will experience.

ER: Motivation Series

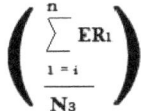

$$\left(\frac{\sum_{1=i}^{n} ER_1}{N_3} \right)$$

-ER (Motivation Series): The motivation series takes into account the factors that impact the personal motivation level of employees to meet organizational objectives. Through the use of increases motivational pathways organizations can improvement upon effort and efficiency.

EF (Innovation)	EM (Employee Motivation)	ES (Employee Satisfaction)
Educational Attainment Recruitment	Employee Goal Setting	Employee Commitment Factor
Exploratory Environmental Research	Performance Feedback	Compensation Equity Factor
Employee Training Quality	Perception of Fairness/Justice	Volunteer Behavior Factor
Idea Sharing Processes	Equity Compensation Factor	Labor-Management Trust Factor
Informational Sharing/Gathering Pathways	Leadership Perception Factor	Positive Group Behavior
Idea Incorporation in Operations/Products/Services	Employee Encouragement Factor	Perception of Organizational Ethics
Problem Solving Teams	Management-Labor Trust Factor	Perception of Leadership Strength
Employee Involvement in Decision Making	Management-Labor Respect Factor	Employee Withdrawal Factor (-)
Individual Incentive/Bonus Plans	Decision-Making Ability Factor	Employee Absenteeism Factor (-)
Group Incentive/Bonus Plans	Perception of Management Quality	Employee Turnover Rates (-)
Employee Mentorship	Positive Group Relationships	Stress and Anxiety Level (-)
Individual/Group Profit Sharing Plans	Employee Recognition Factor	Perception of Organizational Culture
Strength of Employee-Management Communication	Potential Growth Opportunities	Positive Work Environment
Product/Idea to Market Effectiveness	Feelings of Organizational Loyalty	Length of Employment Factor

New Products/Services Offered	Employee Needs Identification	Positive Individual Socialization
ROI on Innovative Projects	Perceptions of Employee Needs Fulfillment	Perceived Discipline Equity
Organizational Innovation Partnerships	Employee Job Importance	Positive Group Socialization
	Employee Task Relevance	Group Goal Attainment
	Environmental Working Conditions	Individual Goal Achievement
	Employee Training Opportunities	Employee Approach Factor
	Employee Communication Networks	
	Employee Task Completion	

Chapter 7
EF: Innovating the Organization
Cogito, Ergo Sum!
(I think, therefore I am!)

Cogito, Ergo Sum!

(I think, therefore I am!)

"Our system though curious and peculiar may be worked safely…if

we wish to work it, we must study it"-Walter Bagehot

Innovation is a necessity in a world where markets are rapidly changing and product life cycles are increasingly shortened. Professor Kanter from Harvard University states, *"In this world of intensified competition organizations can no longer afford to be followers, to wait for somebody else to innovate"* (Knap, 2011). Organizations that desire to create and grow new markets will need to continuously solve problems and create new products for consumer consumption.

Despite its need the definition of innovation can be difficult to pinpoint due to its creative process based deeply in human thought and is thus not well understood even by experts (Gaspersz, 2005). As a general definition industry researchers indicate that innovation is the *"ability of a new product to solve a customer's problem"* (Studt, 2005). The concept of product includes tangible goods, intangible goods like services, or even internalized improvements in operational management.

Such development is necessary if organizations desire to continue to grow in a highly competitive marketplace. At present knowledge workers are quickly becoming the largest employee sector in developed countries (Pot, 2011). Knowledge work focuses on quality above the manufacturing perspective of quantity to achieve its long-term objectives (Drucker, 1999). Once an idea has been fully developed, it can then be adjusted for quantitative manufacturing for economies of scale.

The process of exploring new paths and putting them into practical use is difficult for organizations. It requires the development of an appropriate understanding of how innovation works within the individual, how to foster appropriate processing mechanisms, and the application of such new solutions for practical wealth generation. Understanding how each approach works with the next helps to create a stronger methodology for implementing innovation within the workplace.

Individual Innovation

In order to increase organizational innovation it is necessary to raise the amount of innovative employees and enhance their ability to develop solutions to problems. Before this can happen, it is important to understand how innovation operates within the individual's mind. Thus, the process of innovation becomes an important indicator of the types of problems that can be solved successfully and comprehensively.

Competence in problem solving depends on the number of concepts explored (sequentially and/or in parallel), available knowledge, and context-sensitivity of this information. Thus, problem solving uses many different pathways in finding an appropriate solution. All of these factors depend directly or indirectly on propagation depth (Zoghi, Mohr & Meyer, 2010). In other words, potential solutions are processed through multiple neural networks in order to explore connections of possible outcomes.

Innovation is often associated with intelligence where concrete problems take the form of internal mental processes where possible routes are conceived, explored, and compared. The cognitive process first starts with the conceptualization of the problems definition, what aspects need to change and then exploring avenues that are most likely to solve the problem (Heylighen, 2003). Each of these avenues can be tried within a person's thought processes and then tested within the environment.

Graham Wallas in his work *Art of Thought* believed that innovation comes from 1.) preparation of the problem through informational collection; 2.) incubation of the concept; 3.) intimation of feelings that solutions are coming; 4). illumination of a concept from preconscious processing into consciousness; and 5) verification of the ideas through environment testing (Wallas, 1926). In such a situation, the contextual understanding of a problem requires an exploration based in prior knowledge and then awareness of potential solutions.

People on the path to innovate a new solution may not know they are on the verge of a breakthrough due to the subtle but yet unconscious information they have collected from their environment that is conceptualized through their education frameworks. Yet, once the appropriate connections have been formed feelings may arise before the actual solution is consciously accepted. A single concept may expand out to larger connecting ideas thereby becoming more holistic and effective in its solution.

Personal Innovative Abilities

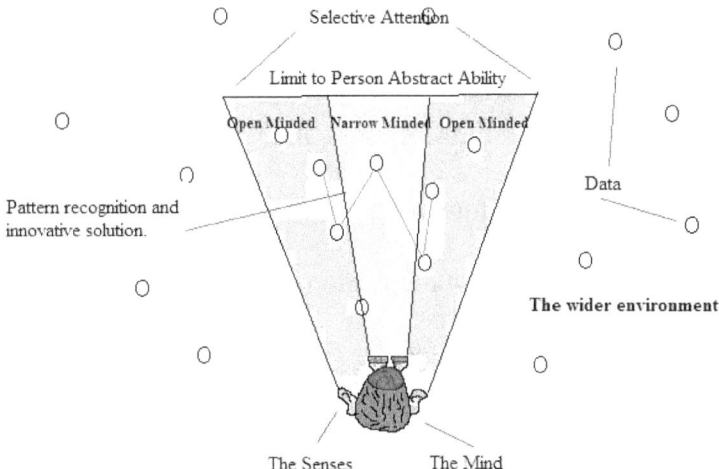

Each person has limited capacity to make meaning and find innovative solutions from data in the environment. Hedging employees skills and enhancing their abilities increase there abilities.

Walla's approach has been adjusted by Helie and Sun into the Explicit-Implicit Interaction (EII) theory of creativity which relies on 1.) co-existence of and differences between explicit and implicit knowledge; 2.) the simultaneous involvement of implicit and explicit processes in tasks; 3). redundant representation of explicit and implicit understandings; 4.) integration of information from explicit and implicit processes; and, 5.) the use of interactive and bidirectional processing (Helie& Sun, 2010). Since potential solutions may not be readily apparent through previous knowledge, the exploration of multiple pathways and environmental factors can work in tandem to find a solution.

Implementing Organizational Innovation

Organizations that desire to improve upon their future growth potential will need to incorporate innovative mechanisms within the workplace. A number of methods exist in which to view the potential improvement and innovation of an organization which includes the performance, competency, and strategy-based perspectives (Chen & Muller, 2010). Possible methods of measuring innovation are as follows:

1.) Performance Perspectives: innovation investment, number/percentage of prior entrepreneurs within the company, percentage of workforce time dedicated to innovative projects, number of products produced, revenue generated from innovative products and improvement of ROI on product lines.

2.) The Competence Perspective: innovative-competence of employees, percentage of employees who received training in innovation, idea generation processes, and informational support for innovation.

3.) The Strategy Perspective: executive time spent on strategic innovation initiatives, amount of innovative ideas incorporated into operations, improvement in revenue and profits as a result of innovative improvements, ratio of submitted ideas versus commercialized ideas.

Research into innovative processes within organizations helps to understand the nature of bubbling concepts that produce meaningful results. Innovative organizations have streamlined their knowledge generation processes in order to limit the loss of ideas within the chaos of daily operations. Organizations that seek to capitalize on their innovative processes should ensure that they reduce conflicting demands and open the process to multiple pathways of idea generation (Bledow, et. al, 2009). Employees, managers and executives are capable of understanding concepts of improvement within the organization and should not be restricted from contributing.

Innovation Through the Conscious and Unconscious

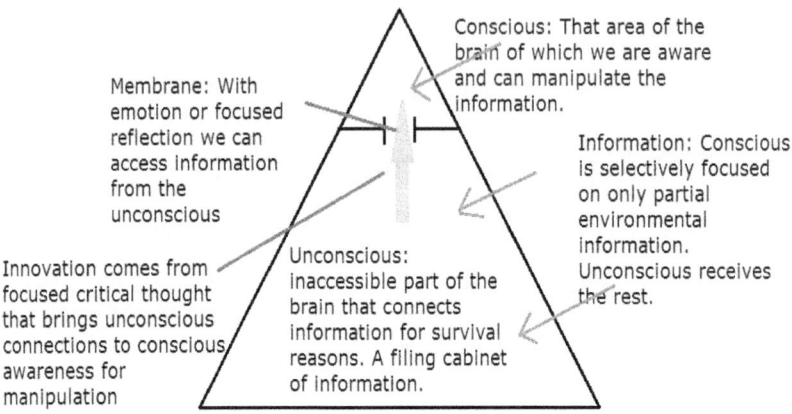

The development of innovation cannot be realized as a separate away from the growth of employees themselves. The development of teams, high levels of employee involvement and an organizational focus on employees in terms of communication are inherent parts of innovative development (Sastry, 2011; Zoghi, Mohr & Meyer, 2010). Employees, who deal with daily problems, may have solutions with no outlet or process to share those solutions.

At Whirlpool the use of embedding innovation into the organization takes the following form (Snyder & Duarte, 2009):

1.) Strategic Architecture: Coordinated actions plans the help foster innovation.

2.) Management Systems: Subsystems within the daily infrastructure that connects behavior and outcomes into employee understanding.

3.) Creation of Idea Pipelines: Development of processes that convert ideas into innovations.

4.) Mentors: The use of mentors to help employees make practical exploration and use of innovations.

5.) Execution and Results: The process of innovating on a particular program will continue as long as the product and service provides measurable benefits in the marketplace.

Creation of innovation within the workplace can often focus on creating teams, commitment to cause, employee involvement, and focus on employees (Sastry, 2011). Teams should afford the opportunity to measure their efforts in terms of patents but also small improvements, higher levels of commitment to the innovative process, involvement of employees in the process, and offering opportunities for employees to display their skills.

The development of new models and inventions within the workplace rely heavily on access to information and the transformation of that information to something useful. This includes the following concepts (Bersin, 2010):

1. Expert teaching model: university and external researchers offer lectures and brainstorming sessions for managers and technical employees.

2. Design and technical teams.

3. Encourage innovative and creative ideas through new expectations.

4. Push for technical skill, collaboration, and innovation.

A study of 698 Australian firms found that those organizations that fostered strong employee-management communication also reported higher levels of innovation (Rogers, 1999). Therefore, innovation is a process of strong communication networks within organizations that share knowledge. Innovation is this sharing of knowledge that helps people to bounce and relate ideas for newer levels of understanding.

Employee suggestion and survey programs, open access to information, and labor-management consultant committees foster innovation (Zoghi, Mohr & Meyer, 2010). The characteristics of such organizations include decentralized decision rights, information-sharing, individual incentive pay plans, group incentive plans, and profit sharing plans. Such organizations appear to balance the inputs of information and shared decisions with motivation and compensation.

Experts suggest hiring divergent thinkers, expecting all employees to problem solve, incentivizing innovative ideas, developing project teams, developing innovation quotas, knowledge sharing and idea borrowing atmosphere, providing time for reflection, and cataloging old ideas can help organizations innovate (Ramsey, 2003). New ideas are fostered through stronger environmental factors that encourage such ideas. These factors help to develop the right amount of work, incentives, and motivation to encourage higher levels of innovative performance.

Innovation and ROI

In order for innovative processes to have practical benefit some level of cost analysis is needed. Benefits compared costs are calculated to produce return on investment that is higher than the cost to implement (Kemp, 2006). Some organizations may consider the use of time to market, new product sales, in addition to Return on Investment (ROI) (Snyder & Duarte, 2009). Thus, innovation requires some level of investment, projected results, and analysis to determine if programs were successfully implemented and beneficial to the organization's goals.

The pipeline of information should transform knowledge into solutions in a measured and systematic way. An organization that is able to innovate is also able to transform knowledge into new ideas that solve problems, develop new processes, and creates new systems (Popa, Preda, and Boldea, 2010). When innovation is effective it should have a measured impact in efficiency, profits, effectiveness or market impact.

How companies allocate their innovative resources has an impact on their ROI. Companies that allocate 70% of their innovative activity to core projects, 20% to adjacent projects, and 10% to transformation projects outperformed other companies and received a price per earning premium of 10-20% (Nagji& Tuff, 2012). Thus when the allocation of resources is not in proportion to the environmental risks and too heavily distorted in favor of transformational projects the rate of financial return declines. Each type of innovation feeds into the development of the next project with transformational being a lead method of discovery but core projects having practical utility.

The development of innovation focuses on the individual, the group, and organizational processes of idea development. One major component cannot be encouraged at the expense of the others. The abilities of employees, their intellectual capacity to develop solutions, and the pathways to that solution should work in tandem for a total positive effect. Innovation is the constant development of viable solutions to problems that result from information, individual development, and organizational development. Through developing the right mixes of elements organizations can further both the abilities of employees and the potential revenue generation opportunities of the organization. Through this revenue generation American organizations can further compete on the global market.

Innovation Sub-factors:

Education Attainment: The level of base knowledge the organization currently carries and recruits within the organization.

Q.) What are the educational attainments, prior knowledge, and skill level currently retained within the organization?

Exploratory Research: The ability of employees to find solutions to problems by exploring environmental problems.

Q.) Are employees free to try new ideas, concepts, and solve problems related to their positions?

Training Quality: This is the training quality offered to employees to increase their skill, understandings, and abilities.

Q.) How would you rate the training quality offered at your organization to meet work requirements?

Idea Sharing: These are the formal and informal processes employees used to share their ideas and solutions to problems.

Q.) How easy is it to share your ideas for improving the business in both formal and informal ways?

Information Sharing Pathways: These are the formal and informal methods employees share and receive information with managers.

Q.) What is the quality level of information being shared both by and to management?

Idea Incorporation in Operations/Products/Services: These are the amount of ideas that are being incorporated into the actual operational, product offerings, or service abilities of the company.

Q.) How successful is the company in using employee ideas and incorporating them into the development of the organization?

Problem Solving Teams: These are the teams, meetings, and committees that are used to provide decision making input into the organization.

Q.) How effective is the company in using teams in developing employee input on organizational decisions?

Individual Incentive Plans: These are the incentive and bonus plans that are offered to employees who solve problems and improve upon the organization.

Q.) How effective are the individual incentives to encourage employees to participate in solving organizational problems?

Group Incentive Plans: These are the incentive and bonus plans that are offered to teams and groups of employees that solve problems and improve upon the organization.

Q.) How effective are the group/team incentives to encourage employees to participate in solving organizational problems?

Employee Mentorship: This factor determines the level and success managers in coaching and mentoring employees.

Q.) How effective are managers in providing accurate coaching and mentoring to employees?

Individual/Group Profit Sharing Plans: This sub-factor helps to encourage a wider understanding that success of the individual and group are tied to the success of the organizational entity.

Q.) What is the quality of the individual or group profit sharing plans?

Employee-Management Communication: These are associated with the ability of employees and managers to communicate and thereby share expectations, tasks, values, and human-to-human bonds.

Q.) What is the quality of communication between employees and managers?

Product/Idea to Market Effectiveness: The success of moving conceptual products to market encourages the financial growth of the organization.

Q.) How effectively does the organization move products/services from the conceptual stage to market actualization?

New Products/Services Offered: The ability of organizations to offer new products and services to capitalize on market needs is important for improving financial revenue streams.

Q.) Does the organization (department) offer an appropriate level of products and services to meet customer/market needs?

ROI on Innovation Projects: This is the effective capitalization on ideas and projects to further business interests.

Q.) How well does the organization maximize opportunities on new ideas and projects?

Chapter 8
ES: Developing Employee Satisfaction
Uva Uvam Vivendo Varia Fit!
(Diverse grapes, through time, grow together).

Uva Uvam Vivendo Varia Fit!
(Diverse grapes, through time, grow together).
The joy in the job comes not so much from the result, not from the

product, but from contributing to optimization of the system in

which everybody wins (Deming as quoted in Orsini, 2013, pp. 200)

Employee satisfaction is more than the gleeful continuity of

worker engagement and productivity. Satisfaction cannot be forced

upon the working population with words like "be thankful for a

job" or slight employment threats of "do you like your job?"

Developing the elusive concepts of employee satisfaction may be

difficult but can create higher levels of organizational efficiency

and return on investment if mastered well. Satisfied employees are

more productive, committed, and loyal to organization needs

without the need for rigid top down management. Furthermore,

such satisfied employees reward their employers with lower labor

costs that can help organizations balance their budgets and

improve future market prospects. Understanding the nature of

employee satisfaction can create opportunities for organizational

improvements that can capitalize on human abilities. As Sam

Walton the founder of Wal-Mart stated "*The essence of*

competitiveness is liberated when we make people believe that what they think and do is important - and then get out of their way while they do it".

Commitment and Labor Costs

Job satisfaction is based upon employee's perceptions and commitment to the work and the organizations where they are employed. When these feelings are positive, higher levels of job satisfaction often bring a number of organizational benefits. Employees, who are satisfied with their jobs, are also likely to be more committed to the organization (Miller & Monge, 1986). This commitment manifests itself through both their workplace social networks and the employer that provides their pay checks.

Highly committed employees exert extra effort to come into work each day despite life's distractions. As employees become more involved it reduces incidents of worker withdrawal and absenteeism (Gadon, 1984). Withdrawal and absenteeism causes labor inefficiencies that can add up and damage the long term profitability of the company. Over time it can destroy a company.

Absenteeism, grievances, and staff turnover are some signs related to a lack of employee satisfaction (McNeese-Smith, 1996). Organizations that desire to reduce these costs should consider the cultural underpinnings associated with resistance type behavior. Employers that develop corporate cultures and incentives which are designed to break down the *Mauer im Kopt* or *Walls of the Mind* also reduce miscommunication and distrust between labor and management. This strong communication process and trust help to create higher levels of efficient engagement that makes it way throughout the employees daily work life.

These walls can be reduced through active listening and strong communication processes. When managers can listen, send appropriate messages, and ensure that such messages are being received properly they can connect with their employees and build stronger relationships that lead to employee satisfaction. The communication process includes the sourcing (speaker), (encoding) taking images and putting them into words (channel) to send to the receiver who (decode) reconstructs the language to create new images. In order to be sure that the proper messages are being sent and received managers should learn to ask for feedback. It is these communicative engagement that lowers encampment and speeds up the efficiency of the workplace.

The Communication Process

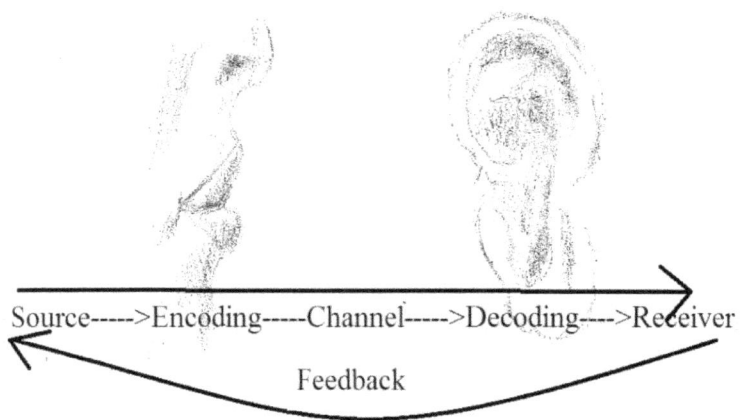

Source----->Encoding-----Channel----->Decoding---->Receiver

Feedback

Half the world is composed of people who have something to say and can't, and the other half who have nothing to say and keep on saying it. - Robert Frost

Compensation

Employee satisfaction may also originate from a feeling of fair compensation for positive worker performance. Some may consider this an expectancy valence dynamic. Worker contributions ultimately make their way into an exchange of effort for organizational rewards (Barnard, 1938). When the rewards do not match the efforts, workers begin to feel a level of dissonance or unfairness. This feeling of unfairness will eventually increase resistance type behavior through work stoppage, absenteeism, and other costly labor reactions.

Yet, compensation is not the only motivating reason why workers engage their environments. Research helps to support the idea that highly satisfied employees are willing to exert additional effort when their supervisors needed help without the immediate benefit of a reward (Berkowsitz, 1972). Workers were not oblivious to the social exchange needed to ensure organizational success. As social creatures, employees were willing to put in time and effort to overcome immediate organizational obstacles and delayed gratification for an appropriate later date.

Huseman and Hatfield (1989) believed that when employees do not earn a return on the investment in proportion to their expended energy they feel stress and anxiety. This stress and anxiety can create dissonance that will lead to higher levels of distrust and disgruntled actions that reduce overall investment returns. Returns are reduced when employees begin to withdraw from the workplace and their fellow workers. They no longer see their goals and the goals of the organization moving in the right direction. Much of these decisions are based in how they consciously understand their work environment and the subconscious makes meaning that lead to disengagement choices.

The conscious and subconscious choice to engage actively in their social groups and the workplace tasks relies on a number of factors. Research in Neuroeconomics helps to highlight the concept that workers make rational choices, based upon their genetic and social development, to rationally seek their own happiness (Fischman, 2012). Employees need to make a rational and willing choice to engage in the betterment of their organizations without coercion if maximum efficiencies are to be found. Thus, engagement is a personal choice fostered by the work environment. The right work environment will foster higher levels of engagement while the wrong work environment will increase personal and professional dissonance.

Norms and Values

The system works best when there is a proper mix of norms, rewards, intrinsic satisfaction, and sentiments which are generated from group relationships (Katz, 1964). Workers seek to contribute to their organizational and social networks in ways that create a positive self-image. They often find meaning in these networks and are motivated to engage when the right mix of elements are present. The success of an organization relies heavily on the need of employees to feel part of the process and important contributors to the organizational welfare.

Such organizational citizenship behavior consists of obedience, participation, and loyalty (Graham, 1989). This type of behavior often includes moral-caring relationships that are transactional and transcend instrumental self-interest. Such relations build a sense of trust that employers and employees have mutual self-interests and similar needs based upon positive communal values.

Employees intuitively understand the rules of engagement and when they feel that this engagement is worth their effort they will show either higher levels of motivation. Much of the problems associated with engagement confusion are based in the communication process that transfers message through organizational networks. From CEO to line supervisor the messages should be consistent to ensure there is little confusion about the expectations and the pathways to success within a particular company.

Such trust and cooperation increases more significantly when reciprocated in kind by employers (Griesinger, 1990). The more social interaction and sharing of rewards the more likely employees will continue to push for higher levels of engagement and involvement. Without this trust there is little reason for ensuring both entities are having their needs fulfilled. What could be a collaborative and mutually beneficial relationship becomes a power struggle of alternative needs fulfillment.

Corporate attention to moral-ethical ideals influence self-reports of satisfaction and perceptions of altruistic and conscientious behavior of co-workers (Organ, 1977). The shared values help to create an environment where the overall value of fair play and mutual expectations abound. American businesses, in particular, rely heavily on the concepts of fair play. When there is unfair and dishonest activity in the process, the benefits of mutual self-interest begin to break down and damage the productivity of the organization.

Employee satisfaction and trust rests on an implied contract that transcends simple legal obligations. This trust factor is derived from a sense of loyalty, cooperation, and participation (Tser-Yieth, Hwang, & Liv, 2012). The more each side engages in these trust-building behaviors the higher the trust level rises. Employers expect their workers to be loyal, cooperate in activities and participate in solutions while employees may in turn expect the employer to treat them humanely, give them opportunities for growth, and share in their needs for development.

Leadership Impact

Transformational leadership involves inspirational motivation, intellectual stimulation and individualized consideration behaviors when putting work into the context of employee's physical, mental, and spiritual needs (Tser-Yieth & Shiuh-Nan, 2012). Such leadership does not only focus on the results but also on how the subtle needs of employees impact that obtainment of organizational results. The skilled transformational leader can understand and adjust these nuances for greater impact.

Think of employee satisfaction in terms of the bonds and relationships that are built among leaders and employees as well as employees among each other. Relationship satisfaction and employee volunteer performances are deeply associated (Moorman, 1993). Employees naturally create groups and it is these groups that help them define who they are and what their level of expected contribution will be. Leaders have an opportunity to define the values of these groups.

Additional benefits exist to employee satisfaction and engagement that move beyond the social aspects and directly into the pockets of investors. Employee engagement can increase profits and reduce expenses through satisfaction, effectiveness and motivation by creating efficiencies through engagement (Maylett & Nielsen, 2012). The more employees enlist in the overall development of the organization the more efficient the company develops through the reduction in the waste in time, material and effort.

Empirical evidence is a bit elusive in such complex arrangements but does result in an imperfect association of wealth generation. For example, unstructured interviews with a sample of 21 senior managers from 16 business organizations discovered that leadership style a.) Enhanced profits through reduced turnover and organizational trust; and b.) Increased in organizations where leaders served the needs of their employees (Jones, 2012). Such leaders enhanced their organizational development and potential for profit through the creation and development positive work relationships and appropriate developmental leadership styles.

Before leadership can harness the power of employee satisfaction they need to rest on some important conclusions related to their leadership style and the latent potential of their employees. Strong leaders can empower their employees and encourage them to make their own decisions (Avolio & Bass, 1995). It is this empowerment spread across a group of employees that creates sub-level efficiencies that are not easily measured with formal human resource approaches.

Tips for Managers

Employee satisfaction is an essential element to the overall success and efficient operation of a business. As globalization encourages additional competition forms of management employers will need to find new efficiencies that do not fit easily into previous simplified mathematical models. The elusive concepts of human behavior and beliefs can further be defined to create higher levels of organizational competitiveness. In the case of employee satisfaction it is the commitment, compensation, group norms, and leadership that encourage organizations to reach new productive heights. Fostering the proper values and perspective of the employee toward the organizational goals will encourage greater levels of commitment to both themselves and their social group. This can only be found in the engagement process associated with strong active listening and formal as well as informal communication process.

Employee Satisfaction Sub-Factors

Employee Goal Setting: Helping employees find goals that are important to them and to the organization can increase commitment to improvement and the organization.

Q: Does the organization help employees define goals that are important to them and the organization?

Performance Feedback: Both formal and informal performance feedback should be accurate and encourage proper self-reflection and skill improvement.

Q: Are employee performance appraisals accurate and help employees understand the development of their skills?

Perception of Fairness/Justice: Employees should trust that discipline will be fairly and equitably distributed.

Q: Are employees disciplinary processes and procedures fairly distributed based upon offense?

Equity Compensation Factor: This factor relates to the perceived equity of compensation. Employees should feel that pay is based upon performance and not on other extra activities such as friendship. Furthermore, pay should be seen as equitable when compared to market demands.

Q: Are employees fairly compensated for the amount of effort and work they must achieve?

Leadership Perception Factor: Employees should feel that organizational leadership has the ability to effectively run the organization.

Q: Do employees feel that organizational leadership skills and abilities are adequate for managing the organization?

Management-Trust Factor: The positive trust and relationship between management and labor should be positive in order to create higher levels of communication and commitment.

Q: Does management create trust-orientated relationship with employees?

Management-Labor Respect Factor: Management and labor should maintain appropriate levels of respect in their interactions in order to break down barriers.

Q: Does management and employees have appropriate levels of respect for each other?

Decision-Making Ability Factor: Employees who feel as though they have some ability to make decisions concerning their work are more likely to feel committed to the organization.

Q: Do employees feel as though they have the ability to participate in the decision-making process related to their work?

Perception of Management Quality: Employees should feel that the competence and abilities of their management group are strong and able to effectively manage their respective areas.

Q: Do employees feel that managers have the ability to effectively manage their areas?

Positive Group Relationships: Employees should feel as though they relate to and are able to feel connected to their work group.

Q: Do employees feel that they have a positive relationship with their coworkers?

Employee Recognition Factor: Employees should feel as though they are a valuable factor within the organization and are recognized for their contributions.

Q: Are employees recognized for their contributions to the organization?

Potential Growth Opportunities: Employees should feel as though they are able to growth with the organization.

Q: Do employees feel as though they can stay and grow with the organization?

Organizational Loyalty: Employees should feel as though they are loyal to the organization and its mission.

Q: Do employees feel as though they are committed to the organization and its mission?

Employee Needs Identification: Employee should feel as though management understands their needs and able to help them fulfill these needs.

Q: Do you feel that employees needs are accurately identified and management makes an attempt to fulfill those needs?

Employee Job Importance: Employee should feel that their jobs are important to the organization and its success.

Q: Do employees feel that their jobs are important to the overall success of the organization?

Employee Task Relevance: Employees work tasks should be relevant to the needs of the department and organization.

Q: Are the tasks employees complete on a daily basis relevant to the needs of the organization?

Environmental Working Conditions: The employee environment should be clean, safe, and free from stress producing agents.

Q: Is the employee environment comfortable, safe, and acceptable for work needs?

Employee Training Needs: Employees should be offered training that encourages higher levels of personal and professional development within their fields of work.

Q: Does the organization offer sufficient employee training opportunities to enhance personal and professional skills?

Employee Communication Networks: Employees should have sufficient networks to obtain information both formally and informally to be more effective in their jobs.

Q: Do employees have sufficient formal and informal networks to obtain information need for the effective completion of their functions?

Employee Task Completion: Employees who are able to be part of the entire process of production will be more satisfied with their contribution to the organization.

Q: Are employee able to see and influence tasks to their completion?

Chapter 9
EM: Developing a Motivating Workplace
Aut Viam Inveniam Aut Faciam!
(I'll either find a way or make one!)

Aut Viam Inveniam Aut Faciam!

(I'll either find a way or make one!)

"If, for most of those citizens present, the United States had proved to be a land of educational and economic opportunity, with almost unparalleled guarantees of free expression, there was, once my mouth shut, not a whiff of acknowledgement, let alone gratitude."-1986 John Updike the Pulitzer Prize winner of *Rabbit is Rich* and *Rabbit at Rest*.

Today's organizations must deal with new trends as rapid product changes, technology adjustments, global competition, new methods of communication, demographic changes, and economic shifts to a service economy move at a faster pace. Organizations can no longer limit themselves to job description criteria to evaluate employee worth as employees are constantly pressured to adjust to an ever changing environment (Raza& Nawaz, 2011). Focusing on older models will slow down the process of change and will ultimately cost organizations in terms of productivity and labor costs. Understanding leading theories on employee motivation will help organizations adjust their policies and procedures in order to create higher levels of achievement and ultimately more profits. Future competitiveness rests on encouraging employees to do more with less while staying engaged in their organizations.

The Character of Employee Motivation

Companies that have the ability to create pathways that encourage motivated employees to grasp onto lines of development is important for creating higher levels of organizational development. Modern organizations should understand how to take employee drive and funnel it through appropriate organizational channels (Radovanovic & Savic, 2012). These channels are typically defined in the processes, procedures, and promotional networks of the organization. The stronger and more clear the pathways are defined the more motivational potentials of employees will be drawn to such approaches.

It is beneficial to first understand what motivation is before moving onto a discussion on how to motivate employees within the workplace. Motivation is the set of processes used in defining the goals of behavior. It is this set of processes that support, guide, and maintain the behavior of people, aimed at achieving a particular goal (Radovanovic & Savic, 2012). Thus, motivation is the activity of an employee defining a goal and putting forth energy to obtain it.

Motivation is derived from the word *motivate* which means to push, move, or influence the environment to achieve some objective (Kalimullah et al, 2010). Motivation can also be seen as the process by which behavior obtains a result, attempts to complete an objective and continues to push forward until that objective is completed. It still may further be viewed as an internal drive that pushes to fulfill some want (Bedeian, 1993).

In the workplace, motivation is the essential driving element of the entire business. Workers will come to work, put forth effort, and try to achieve certain goals. Such practical utility and persistence of such behavior requires motivation. Likewise, it is motivation that helps employees follow workplace rules, solve practical problems, and further the organizations interests. From productivity to quality motivation is an essential element of employee efforts. Managers have the ability to foster motivation in employees in order to push them to more productive ends.

As the world market changes organizations should learn to change their approaches to employee management in order to align their organization efforts to environmental realities. The time when employers looked exclusively at job descriptions for measurement of employees' value is over and organizations should now look more closely to individual skills and abilities (Raza& Nawaz, 2011). In the past job based approaches stressed how employees should complete jobs through specific work activities, obligations and accountability (Lawler, 1993). In today's world, employees moved between the grey lines of job descriptions to fulfill every changing tasks.

In modern times a greater emphasis should be placed on the individual that focuses on skills, competencies and abilities (Lawler, Mohrman, & Ledford, 1992). This new perspective creates a dynamic shift from the function of the job to the enhancement of the individual in order to achieve organizational objectives. The more enhanced the individual's abilities the more they can benefit the organization through positive action while weathering environmental difficulties.

Employee motivation is one of the main functions of management that is supported the policies and procedures of an organization (Shadare et al, 2009). Managers have an ethical and moral responsibility to encourage employees to perform to their highest levels. The responsibilities can be codified into the processes, procedures, policies, compensation and other corporate approaches to employee management. By doing so they are fulfilling the fiduciary responsibilities of their positions and contributing to economic growth of both the organization and the nation.

The responsibility of corporate growth does not end with the manager. It also includes employee's responsibility to engage the organization. Through the need to accomplish some goal, or find a path to personal development, an employee will scan their work environment to put their skills, knowledge and abilities to the most appropriate efforts. Such excited employees are seeking ways to make their work more interesting and efficient and therefore organizations should foster this effort in order to make the company more successful (Kalimullah et al, 2010). It this type of scanning and resulting problem solving that ultimately leads to efficiency of effort and higher pay and profits.

Through the capitalization of employee motivation, an organization can meet customer demands, lower costs, and adjust to overcome environmental challenges. Organizational effectiveness is the efficient process of turning inputs into outputs (Matthew et al, 2005). The more efficiently the organization is run through motivating processes the more effective is the process of converting the organizational factors into viable products or services. This is accomplished through the minds and bodies of workers that engage in the micro and macro decisions throughout the entire process.

Precisely what causes one person to be motivated and another to not be motivated is complex. Motivation has a number of factors and contributors that create the right environment for action. *"The complex of forces that initiate and keep somebody at work in a company, this is, the motivation starts and maintain activity in the intended direction*" (Vroom, 1964). Motivation starts within the individual and is maintained through the needs, desires, and benefits of that individual. However, the contextual factors create additional benefits or detractors from their decision to take a certain course of action.

An organization that has a high level of motivated employees is likely to accomplish more goals than those who do not. The organization is considered a socio-economic group that fosters employee motivation in order to earn more revenue as well as weather environmental challenges (Kvedaravicius, 2005). Furthermore, motivation exists within a cultural perspective that impacts its manifestation within the workplace (Savareike, 2011). It is this motivational energy that creates a level of dynamism within an organization which furthers organizational development.

Motivation is a complex process that creates a need and desire within individuals who seek to find paths within the organization to achieve satisfactory fulfillment of these needs and desires. Organizations that can create appropriate pathways for employees to obtain needs fulfillment are likely to maintain higher levels of motivation and reap the financial rewards of higher employee effort. The characteristics and dynamics of motivation exist within a culture perspective of the value of certain needs and can be encouraged through stronger organizational cultures. Moving from a perspective of job tasks to employee centered abilities helps foster a proper framework for understanding employee motivation. Through proper adjustments in the environment and culture an employee is more likely to make the important connection between effort and reward.

Motivational Theories

It is often beneficial to review common motivational theories as they fit within the context of the workplace. Each theory has a particular approach that can lead to greater insight of how motivation works within individuals and the organization in general. Furthermore, each theory also has a different vantage point that rests in psychological development, workplace opportunities, goal orientation, or social expectations. Consider the following theories:

Maslow Hierarchy of Needs: Through this theory the needs of individual's progress through different stages based upon their development. People move through physiological needs, security and safety, social needs, self-esteem and self-actualization. As each person accomplishes some need the next one takes precedence.

Frederick Herzberg's Two Factors Theory: In this theory there are primarily two factors of satisfied and dissatisfied. Satisfaction often came through the context of work functions while dissatisfaction was often a result of the organizational dynamics. Motivation fosters the execution of work tasks while the organizational factors were seen as context to these factors.

Theory X and Theory Y: In such a theory the X employee has a low level of motivation and the Y is engaged in the work task. The X employee does not feel as though the environment should make particular demand while the Y employee feels that such demands are a normal part of work life. X employees must often be coerced while Y employees have a more natural tendency to engage in the work environment.

The Expectancy Theory: Developed by Vroom (1964) and Porter & Lawler (1968) as a way of understanding individual motivations within the workplace. According to the theory each employee has expectancies of their work environment. When the expectancies are in match with work performance and clear rewards from the environment the employee will create motivation.

The Goal Setting Theory: The theory helps explain that setting goals and having appropriate feedback creates higher levels of motivation (Latham &Locke, 1979). Organizations can partner with individuals to help those set goals that are acceptable to the company and continue to give them accurate performance feedback throughout employees' fulfillment of these processes.

Equity Theory: The equity theory indicates that motivation is a result of how people are treated when compared to others. In this theory people are more motivated when there is a perception of fairness and just treatment of everyone. Employees view the rewards of others and their distribution patterns to determine if they are being treated fairly for their efforts.

The Group Culture Theory: Even when dealing with individuals it is important to consider the factors that motivate an entire group that may have needs that are distinctly different from those of the individual. Under this theory the personality of a group and their needs should be considered as a motivational factor (Adair, 2006).

Me-conomics Theory: Our most basic purchase motivations are for the biological protection. We work for the purchasing of basic clothing, food, and shelter. Our motivations to work and obtain products starts with basic physiological needs, develops to social endeavors, and then to self-expression. At the highest level our work and purchases are more self-expressive. Each level of development doesn't destroy the achievements of the lower two economic identities but capitalizes on them to a greater extent by putting them within their proper perspectives. Motivation is based on the need to take care of one self and purchase products.

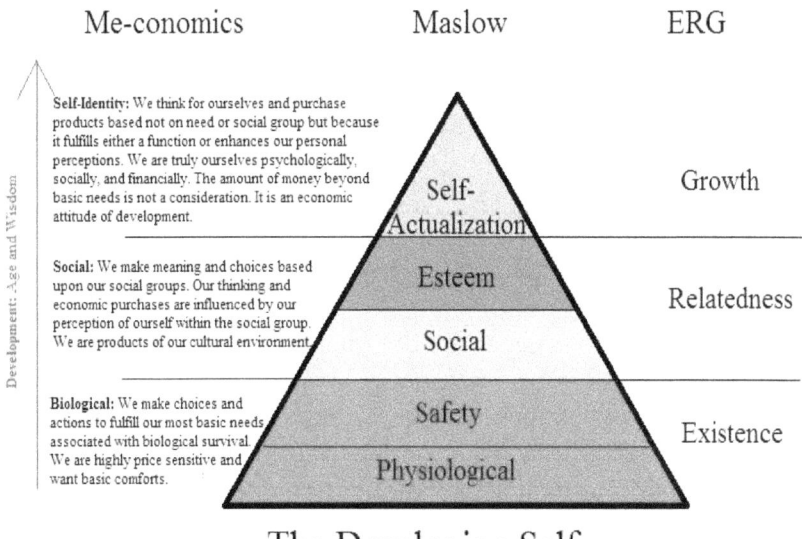

Me-conomics   Maslow   ERG

Development: Age and Wisdom

Self-Identity: We think for ourselves and purchase products based not on need or social group but because it fulfills either a function or enhances our personal perceptions. We are truly ourselves psychologically, socially, and financially. The amount of money beyond basic needs is not a consideration. It is an economic attitude of development.

Social: We make meaning and choices based upon our social groups. Our thinking and economic purchases are influenced by our perception of ourself within the social group. We are products of our cultural environment.

Biological: We make choices and actions to fulfill our most basic needs associated with biological survival. We are highly price sensitive and want basic comforts.

Self-Actualization — Growth

Esteem

Social — Relatedness

Safety

Physiological — Existence

The Developing Self

Within each of these theories there is an opportunity to see the overall categories of employees and how they approach their environments. Understanding how the employee behaves within the environment further highlights their particular interest and approaches. Managers can use these interests and approaches to make important decisions on the motivational vehicles they would like to offer employees. The motivational type of the employee often impacts his or her vantage point and choices. As a the person matures and develops their choices, economic assumptions and motivations also mature and change.

Motivational Types

Even though understanding the common theories is helpful to create an encompassing view of motivation as it does not address the behavioral methodologies employees use to put forth energy in their environment. The theories help us understand how motivation develops while the types categorize the general make up of the individuals that display motivational tendencies. It is these genres that help managers understand how certain individuals relate to their environment. There are four positive motivational types and one negative type that impacts employee behavior (Gerchirov, 2005 & 2008):

Instrumental Type: Workers who actively orientate toward earning money as a way of satisfying all of their needs.

Professional Type: Workers who seek self-realization through the context of employment. They desire to use abilities, active involvement and initiative, improve qualifications and engage in creativity.

Patriotic Type: Workers who seek collective engagement, team work, interaction with colleagues, work relations, and finding common causes.

Take Charge Type: Workers who desire maximum independence, reject control, and have purposeful orientation of action.

Avoidance Type: Workers who engage in negative behavior this is designed to reduce effort, focus on self gain, follows rigid traditions and avoids responsibility.

Each of these motivational types impacts the methods employees use to navigate their environment. For example, some employees may seek to obtain financial resources as a main motivational schema while another seeks to gain new skills and abilities. Understanding the motivational type of each employee can help to foster more motivational approaches and efforts in engagement. Managers should seek to determine the appropriate motivational theory and motivational type in order to align their approaches to the needs of their employees.

Herzberg's 2-Factor Motivational Theory

One of the more commonly used and practical theories is Herzberg's 2-Factor Motivational Theory which proposes that employee motivation is a result of internal and external incentives. Research in Lithuania furthers the concepts by finding that the three motivating factors for employee's efforts lay in personal achievement, the type of work and personal development (Balvociute & Bakanauskien, 2011). The study highlights how the internal need to achieve and develop leads to the external motivational behaviors that engage the work environment. The combination of the two factors can further lead to higher wages and income.

There is also another way to apply these two concepts. According to the EFQM-Model, measurements of motivation encompass enablers and results. Specific enablers include leadership, people, policy & strategy, partnership & resources, and processes while the results are often exhibited in people, customer, society and other key performance metrics (Ehrlich, 2006). In other words, the motivating pathways lead to specific performance outcomes that are reinforced through reward. It is the combination of these employee efforts that increases the organizations financial success.

Motivation is difficult to maintain unless there is some satisfaction level obtained by employees. According to Bruggmann (1974) satisfaction can be seen in three different processes that include expectations, level of aspiration, and problem solving. Employees use these three different processes when evaluating whether or not they are going to exert effort on some objective. If they cannot find a solution to their expectations or aspirations they may not engage in motivated behaviors.

Motivational potentials are those organizational pathways that encourage employees to latch to a line of development. Such motivational potentials often reside in the conditions of defined areas of responsibility, definitions of optimal work results, positive work tasks, results of sub-dominant goals, transparent incentive systems, and opportunities of choice of rewards (Heckhausen & Rheinberg, 1980). Before employees are motivated to fulfill certain needs they will want the right environment with appropriate potentials for success.

Job Motivational Field

It can be beneficial to see job motivation as a field where intrinsic and extrinsic forces influence a person to act in a particular scope or direction (Savareikiene, 2012). It is also possible to predict these behaviors based upon these pressures. For example, an employee who is highly motivated to achieve some objective and perceives a rewarding path will likely do so if the right factors are present. The job motivational field can be expanded through job enrichment tactics.

Through expanding employees desires to learn new skills and achieve it is often beneficial to engage in job enrichment. Job enrichment is a qualitative change to employment that increases autonomy, accurate feedback, job significance, and influence on their work environments (Hackman & Oldham, 1976). Job enrichment encourages workers to learn, develop, and innovate solutions which further morale and satisfaction (Hackman & Lawler, 1971). As the employee learns higher levels of work mastery in a variety of arenas they become more capable in their abilities, more knowledgeable of their environment, and take greater ownership of their work. It is this knowledge that they alone are responsible for their work and have ownership of their results that leads to greater motivation (Orpen, 1979).

A survey of 534 respondents indicated that job enrichment was associated with job motivation, job satisfaction and mildly with organizational commitment (Raza& Nawaz, 2011). The study further helps cement the ideas that motivation, satisfaction and commitment are associated with mastery over ones work, autonomy, and greater knowledge of the work environment. The path to higher levels of motivation rests, in part, in the development of workers through appropriate training and development which leads to general enrichment of their capabilities.

Approach and Avoidance Motivation in Creative Individuals

Creative individuals are considered an asset to organizations that seek to develop new ideas and market approaches. Such creativity encourages higher performing artists and scientists when compared to average colleagues that do not have the same level of creativity (Csikszentmihalyi, 1996). Such people simply perform at a higher level and are able to come up with more unique solutions that their counterparts cannot.

Organizations face all types of environmental events in a global market and will need to capitalize on such creativity in order to overcome these challenges. Research indicates that creative individuals are better able to solve complex problems and manage social situations (De Dreu & Nijstad, 2008). This means that their abilities give them unique advantages in the world of work and life.

New research has come to light that helps us understand why between two creative individuals one will perform at a high level and the other will not. The research conducted by Roskes, De Drue and Nijstad helps organizational leaders understand the differences between approach and avoidant type creative individuals and how this impacts their output. It also further discusses how approach type creative people are more focused on goals and use less energy in achieving them.

Creativity can be defined as the generation of ideas, understandings and solutions that have useful outcomes (Hennessey & Amabile, 2010). Creative people use goals in order to keep their focus and creative energy in an effort to attain particular outcomes (Austin & Vancouver, 1996). It is through the generation of new approaches and desired results that motivates creative individuals to achieve their goals.

A predictor of creativity in the workplace is the desire to use approach motivation, versus avoidance motivation, to engage potential positive outcomes (Mehta & Zhu, 2009). The duel-pathway model to creativity indicates that such people engage in both cognitive flexibility as well as cognitive persistence. This means that creative people are more willing to engage potential outcomes and use both flexibility and persistence to achieve their goals.

The use of fluid, divergent, and flexible approaches that leads to higher levels of creative outcomes (Oppenheimer, 2008). Such creative people often focus on the positive outcomes and seek multiple paths from many perspectives in order to find appropriate connections of relevant information to determine a potential solution. Through this higher level of processing creative people can develop additional solutions that outperform their colleagues.

A study conducted by Roskes, De Drue and Nijstad (2012) attempted to determine avoidance and approach orientated mental processes of creativity. A series of five different studies were conducted on students and further helped to determine the overall costs and benefits of each style. The research helps highlight some key findings that are beneficial in innovative markets:

-Avoidance motivated individuals used much more energy when compared to approach motivated people.

-Approach motivated individuals found tasks easier than avoidance motivated individuals.

-Approach motivated individuals maintained their effort with near goal completion feedback while avoidance motivated people reduced their effort.

-Approach motivated individuals engaged more in the process of being creative while avoidance-motivated individuals focused more on the achievement of the goal.

-Avoidance motivated individuals suffer more from cognitive loads in their working memory than approach motivated people.

The results helps leaders understand the creative individuals that have learned to approach problems and the potential outcomes tackle problems using all of their abilities. This means that they not only do not shy away from challenge but have more mental faculties and approaches to finding solutions. Such individuals are also able to have higher levels of energetic performance because they use less energy in their mental faculties. They are persistent, efficient, flexible, and competent.

Components of Motivation

The Legitimacy Model views organizational effectiveness as *"component preferences for performance and natural limitations on performance from an external environmental perspective"* (Zammuto, 1982). In other words, while reviewing an organization it is possible to determine its effectiveness by understanding employees' preferences for performance and the limitations these employees have in utilizing these pathways. If road blocks are removed employees will put their effort toward those designed pathways which have the highest chance of success.

Leadership is an essential component of motivation. Through employee trust of management they will believe that the leadership function of the organization will fulfill their explicit and implicit promises (Baldoni, 2005). Thus, leadership and trust in management is necessary if employees are to make that decision to put forward effort into the organizational pathways. The leadership function and the labor function raise each other to higher levels of motivation and morality in a synergistic manner that furthers market interests (Rukhmani, Ramesh, &Jayakrishnan, 2010).

The essential components of employee motivation rely in trust, rewards, decision making, empowerment, information and group expectations (Adeyinka et al., 2007; Baldoni, 2005; Brewer et al., 2000; Hassan et al., 2011;Yazdaniet al., 2011;). When these components work in tandem an environment can be more aligned to the needs of the employees and thus produce more meaningful results for the organization. Investors should ensure their management teams are working to continually align their organizations to foster these motivational components to meet environmental needs.

Summary Suggestions for Management

From the literature, managers can learn a number of important concepts that benefit employees and their organizations. Through the development of the employee, the organization can realize higher levels profit return while reducing overall labor costs through less need for powerful structural controls on behavior. Furthermore, offering pathways for development will give employees more opportunities to be motivated. Motivation, self-interest, and self-development is first generated in the individual and then manifested within the organization. Such development strengthens the overall future prospects of both the organization and the individual in order to ensure there is greater ability to adjust to market changes. Highly creative individuals are motivated from the task and process and expend less effort in finding solutions by actively engaging problems. The ultimate goal of any organization is to encourage active engagement of organizational problems and solutions to market needs. A new way of looking at the employee and their potential within the organization can create a better vantage point by changing from a perspective of the job function to the capabilities of the employee. That capacity to both understand and develop is rooted in employees biological, social, and self-identity needs.

Motivation Sub-Factors

Employee Commitment Factor: Employees should feel committed to the organization. Such commitment has an impact on disciplinary, retention, commitment, and motivation.

Q: Do employees have a commitment to the organization and its mission?

Compensation Equity Factor: Employees should feel as though they are fairly compensated based upon their efforts.

Q: Do employees feel as though they are fairly compensated for the work effort they put forward?

Volunteer Behavior Factor: Employees who engage in volunteer behavior also maintain higher levels of motivation than those who don't.

Q: Do employees regularly engage in volunteer behavior both within and outside the organization?

Labor-Management Trust Factor: The more trust managers and labor have with each the more connected and inclusive of decisions. How the managers and employees view each other impacts how much effort will be put forward.

Q: What is the trust level between employees and managers?

Positive Group Behavior: Employees should feel connected and associated with their workplace group.

Q: Do employees feel they have positive relationships with other employees?

Perception of Organizational Ethics: Employees should feel as though their organization operates in an ethical and fair manner that encourages appropriate rules that apply to all members.

Q: Do employees feel that the organization operates in an ethical and fair manner?

Employee Withdrawal Factor (-1): Employee withdrawal is lower when they feel they are connected and contributing to the organization.

Q: Do employees feel as though they have a contribution to make in the organization?

Employee Absenteeism Factor (-): Employees who are motivated and committed to the organization are more likely to come to work on a consistent basis.

Q: Is the employee absenteeism rate high?

Stress and Anxiety Level (-): Employees who are motivated are likely to feel less stress and anxiety in the workplace.

Q: What is the level of stress and anxiety employees feel within the workplace?

Perception of Organizational Culture: Employees should feel that the organizational culture encourages higher levels of motivation and achievement.

Q: Do employees perceive the organizational culture as a both motivating and encouraging of higher performance?

Positive Work Environment: Employee should work within positive work environments that encourage performance.

Q: Do employees perceive their work environment as positive?

Length of Employment Factor: The organization should not be encouraging highly motivated employees to obtain other jobs in order to achieve their goals.

Q: Do employees feel that they can achieve their long-term goals within the organization?

Perceived Discipline Equity: Employees should feel that their organization used the disciplinary process in a consistent manner that ensures rules are applied uniformly to organizational members.

Q: Do employees feel that the disciplinary process is fair and equitable?

Positive Individual Socialization: Employees should be positively socialized into the norms, expectations and workgroup.

Q: Are employees properly socialized into the norms and expectations of the organization?

Individual Goal Achievement: Employees should feel individually motivated to achieve their goals.

Q: Do employees feel motivated to achieve their personal goals within the workplace?

Group Goal Attainment: Employees should be motivated to achieve group goals for the benefit of themselves and their group.

Q: How important do employees feel it is to achieve group goals?

Employee Approach Factor: Employees should feel free and motivated to actively engage organizational problems for find new solutions.

Q: Are employee free to actively engage and find solutions to problems within the organization?

Chapter 10
Conclusion
Entitas Ipsa Involvit Aptitudinem ad Extorquendum Certum Assensum
(Reality involves a power to compel sure assent)

Entitas Ipsa Involvit Aptitudinem ad Extorquendum Certum Assensum

(Reality involves a power to compel sure assent)

Classic economic theory, based as it is on an inadequate theory of human motivation, could be revolutionized by accepting the reality of higher human needs, including the impulse to self actualization and the love for the highest values.-Abraham Maslow

Developing strong organizations requires the creation of a system that not only improves value by using organizational processes to finish products but also seeks to enhance those products for consumer consumption. This enhancement can only be successfully found in the intellectual efforts of employees that constantly develop both costs saving and cost generating ideas. These improvements can be seen in product/service enhancements or the development in human ability. Since organizations are socio-economic groups, it is necessary for business leaders to develop their systems appropriately to create the greatest value for themselves, their customers and their employees. Organizational culture enhances organizational learn and market adaptability. The improvement of the business environment also improves the lives or workers and contributes to the national cause of economic prosperity and social influence. Putting Americans to work in ways that are advantageous to society creates new momentum in national improvement and development.

No matter how sophisticated or efficient an organization becomes it is the intellectual capacity of workers that provides future opportunities for growth by creating value beyond systematic constraints. Machines are cold mechanical assembly dragons but do not invent new product streams or new methods of producing value and are thus are limited to their designers imagination. They are, by their nature, confined to the limits of the human mind and its ability to be inventive to enhance production tools.

All economic systems convert inputs to outputs for public consumption. It is this public consumption funneled through the purchases of customers which creates revenue and value. The more efficient and progressive the production system the more likely it will produce value enhancing outputs that raise profits. As products are assembled and manufactured it are the efforts of labor that eventual produce value. This effort can be seen through individual ideation or collective improvement in efficiency and development. It is a process of continually climbing the mountain inch by inch through continuous improvement and upward trajectory.

Economics, efficiency experts, and theorists have come up with varying methodologies to fix or improve upon the production aspects of organizations. They focus on the particular elements to improve the general output. Yet ultimately, all of these improvements are related to the wide lens value of outputs through methods of advancement seen in processes, management styles, human resources, communications, supplier relationships, marketing and all other components of the conversion system; it is this total value that is sold on the market for a profit.

To see an organization as an economic system (i.e. company) within a larger system (i.e. economy) that produces products on the market requires taking a distant viewpoint of the organization in its natural economic environment. To understand the conversion process one should look at it from all of its flowing parts to create understanding on how each of the pieces work together. Ultimately what comes in from the side doors must come out the front door and sold to willing consumers. Every aspect of the organization should be designed to contribute more than its cost in this conversion of input to output process. Where direct cost analysis cannot be seen the qualitative side of enhancement should not be discounted. Analysis and research allows for the ability to review the total process as well as its elemental parts.

Each of these organizational systems also influences to the economic health of the nation and creates sustainability for a culture and a nation. As businesses decline in health so does the revenue of a nation and the future viability of its people. As businesses improve their performance within political, economic, financial and cultural contexts so does the opportunities of a nation to seek additional levels of improvement. Its success provides greater theoretical proof of the viability of a particular cultural vantage point and methodology of influence. Seeing the nature of people, business, culture, and government as separate entities may create more insight into individual in-line characteristics but ignores the contextual influence of its existence as a total living and breathing organism.

Just like in organizations, nations that can align all of the parts together into an efficient machine are able to produce products and services on an international scale that exceeds the competition. The nature of good governance is to create the right cultural, financial, and political atmosphere for both the individual and business to succeed together. Any step away from this focal point of business-people elemental improvements means that other factors have contributed to the political decision-making process that deters from the health and sustainability of the entire system.

For example, spending money on governmental functions that do not have some impact on enhancing and improving the innovative and productive abilities of the people and their employing organizations is money that is thrown in self-serving causes. All aspects of governance are and should be about enhancing the ability of people to succeed on the international market through the manifestation of their abilities. Organizations provide the medium by which people impact their global environment and fulfill their dreams, wishes, and inner most desires. Government should help create the atmosphere to capitalize on the hopes and dreams of people in order to create sustainable societies. It is those hopes and dreams that change reality in the present, redefines the context of the past and creates a future.

Such a focal point would require a new way of thinking about the purpose of government and decision-making. As the nation begins to suffer from the weight of its own infrastructure and poor financial performance the concepts of selfless determination will become more important determinants of change. At the very core of human existence is the furthering of collective self-interest through the development of the entire economic chain. Each piece, whether an individual or an organization, is a small grain of sand that contributes to the success of the entire system. History has taught us that together sand can stop the flood of decline or the bullets of an ever changing world. We must only believe and act in ways the further our societal interests.

This collective conscious and nature of economics is why motivation, innovation and satisfaction are essential components of enhanced human capacity. Whether we are discussing the individual, the organization, or the economy each component should be in alignment to create synergy so that they enhance each other. Motivation ensures force, satisfaction provides stability, and innovation creates solutions to problems. The development of American potential rises from that desire to succeed, the stability of purpose, and the ability to overcome market challenges. The removal of any of the three factors limits the potential of the other two.

Stream of Collective Conscious
A trajectory of thought.

Individual Stream: Understandings of past, present and future of individuals outside of standard cultural understandings. The outliers.

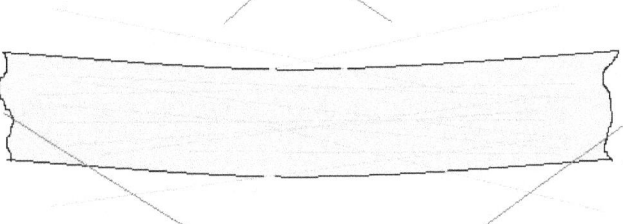

Collective Stream of Conscious: A totality of sequence of images in the populations perceptions that determine the type of decisions made, the probable courses of actions, and potential future of a nation. Each new decision is relative to the decisions made in the past. These images determine who is elected, what projects are supported, and what values a nation will have. Corporations, like nations, have these same streams of cultural understandings, abilities, experiences, and decision making that prime future decisions based upon meaning making of the population and leaders.

This collective conscious is created from our past experiences and the way we interpret new information in our environment to project what the future will likely be. Through our past work and life experiences, we making meaning out of current events to determine appropriate efforts. Understanding employees past understandings and being aware of how they are interpreting new information helps in adjusting that thought process to make proper projections that are most beneficial to themselves and the organization. It is through an alignment of new information from the environment in ways that help employees make meaning which further helps them developing strategies that help the organization and nation succeed.

It is through this proper balance of environmental attributes and national pushes for human development that strong countries can become supreme entities which can balance their budgets and increase global influence. It is the race for the brain that takes precedence in today's world to overcome pricing difficulties and declining exports. To move to the highest forms of human development that encourages collective improvement on the economic food chain and encourages compounding benefits requires singularity of governmental purpose. That purpose rests in creating the right business environment that empowers people and promotes growth within the context of societal benefits that allows citizens to take one step up if they so desire.

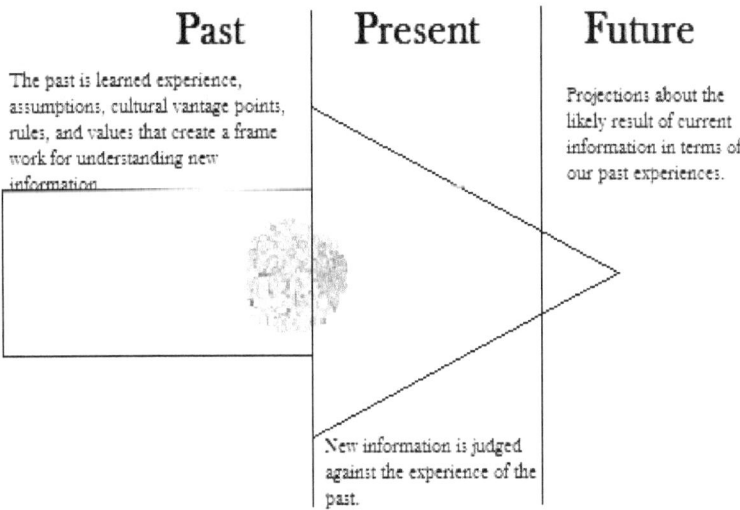

Past | Present | Future

The past is learned experience, assumptions, cultural vantage points, rules, and values that create a frame work for understanding new information.

Projections about the likely result of current information in terms of our past experiences.

New information is judged against the experience of the past.

Deeply embedded beneath all of the fallacies we have learned in our lives, passed from generation to generation, about our place in society we have an innate desire to contribute to the survival of our species in ways that we are best capable. It has programmed into our very biological nature with each function of the body contributing to this fulfillment. Awareness of this need allows businesses and employees to view their development as a moral and ethical fulfillment of human destiny and enhancement of society. When people are able to develop themselves their business entities become pathways to success that offers additional revenue to shareholders. It is these shareholders that reinvest their earned revenues into new business approaches creating a sustainable governmental and economic system that perpetuates upward.

The race to the mind can only occur by breaking through the false constructs we have layered upon each other in human understanding through years of socialization to particular societal orders and understandings. Each human being should be seen as having a purpose in the contribution to the success of the entire system. The fulfillment of self-interest can be properly funneled through organizations and individual endeavors to the fulfillment of collective interests. They are not mutually exclusive concepts and should not be considered antithetical. A system simply cannot function well with the parts pulling in opposite directions and focusing on different root goals and assumptions. We all rise together or fall together in our development regardless of our particular ideological belief systems.

Without this understanding of societal output, the social structure people find themselves embedded within, and the human ability to contribute to collective improvement you would find that many of the functions we engage in are without practical benefit. For example, what is the purpose of primary, secondary, and higher education if it is only the fulfillment of personal need without a contribution to the development of society? Is there any use in flooding the market with new products and services that neither contributes to human development or the development of society?

Innovative problem solving contributes to the success of the individual and their society by offering solutions. As the economic chain creates alignment, solves problems, and contributes to society it develops creative utility that enhances the ability to both generate and obtain wealth. The rewards gained from such contributions should be directly seen in the pockets of individuals and investment coffers in a fair, equitable, and practical manner. The most efficient systems offer opportunities and equity to each for maximum growth and social stability.

The key is to create the right pieces of information that allow for the development of workers abilities by developing strong social interactions, rewards, and available paths that push such workers to more beneficial and productive actions. Of course this cannot happen unless the executives and strategic decision-makers of the organization understand the benefits of creating this proper environment for ethical and profit-drive reasons. If they seek only personal gain they will create resistance by the other elements who also seek to manipulate the system for personal advantage. In the long run conflict will destroy the benefits through social upheaval and resentment. Gain cannot be found through constant conflict and resistance.

Organizations that stifle information and eventually fail to provide for strong training force employees to find meaning from their interactions with other workers. When these social networks have incorrect information they perpetuate less productive behavior. Such actions will often push such workers to view management as untrustworthy due to the lack of transparency in important decisions that impact their working lives. This division of information and perception creates divisions of labor fostered by improper perspectives and sets the organization up for lackluster profits and higher levels of conflict. It becomes an in-group and out-group dynamic that makes its way like a virus through the entire company filling all of the cracks where clear information is not present.

The path forward is not an easy one. It is full of trials, drama, and tribulation that test the resolve of those who desire to see higher performance and the manifestation of American destiny. There will be some who reject their own improvement and will find adequate support among their peers to maintain their disassociation. Their obstructionist views are a direct result of their lack of understanding and poor education to higher sets of values that benefit both themselves and the societies they live within.

Through consistency in information provided from education, families, their social groups, work environments and their governmental representation such obstructionist groups will increasingly become smaller and smaller as well as less able to influence their environment as their ability to adjust institutional order weakens. The more people who adhere to the power of enlightenment the less ignorance will be able to negatively influence that environment. Progressive and positive thinking is logical and beneficial for a nation that seeks to turn the tide of decline. When progressive behavior is embedded into society those who do not follow the new social order will experience resistance and loss of status. Their methodologies are thoroughly evaluated and disregarded as not beneficial.

It is through the understanding of personal and social development that our societal structure adjusts the very way in which we perceived meaning creating a stream of conscious that leads people to proper and logical perceptions of their environment. Shared consciousness of purpose enhances the success of the individual, the organization, and the nation. With adequate social support individuals can continue to emulate perspectives of growth from generation to generation. It is through this race for the mind, and how it makes meaning, that the socialized self can be adjusted for a greater end.

Successful societies are able to create trust between those who govern and those who do the governing. They are able to develop greater economies by aligning both the structure of society as well as the abilities of people to develop themselves as well as society to higher levels of output. It is about creating shared understandings that fosters the proper image construction that helps employees use to make appropriate meaning and purpose of their working lives. It is this meaning employees use to make daily economic decisions that add up to a lifetime legacy.

The path to individual, organizational, and societal freedom and sustainability rests with the ability to tackle the human mind and it's potential. It requires a new way of thinking about man's place and purpose in the world. People must learn that they exist in a social network and that each act they commit influences all other entities of that network. Those in power create a chain of understanding that can lead people to ignorance or enlightenment. Democracy and management should be based on allowing those with the greatest skills to rise in rank due to their ability to positively influence the environment around them. Failures to reign in those societal factors that damage personal and professional growth are failures of societal proportions. As organizations seek additional profits in a world of high technology and constant change they will need to encourage the abilities of their workers on a new level yet unseen on a national scale.

Concluding Concepts

Individual, Organizational and National Development are Interrelated: Employees are part of a larger economic system by which they draw their sustenance and contribute to the development of their society. Organizations have an ethical and business imperative to develop employees to their highest capabilities in order to maximize human capital on a national level. Through the development of the individual, an organization, and a nation they are able to realize higher levels of proficiency, profits, and fiscal responsibility.

Innovation, Employee Satisfaction, and Motivation: Through the encouragement of the innovative, satisfied and motivated employee, a higher level of organizational attainment can be found. Innovation provides utility through problem solving, satisfaction creates stability, and motivation provides the energy needed to overcome market challenges. It is through this diatribe of factors that an organization can run as an ethical yet efficient machine with the capacity to raise human capital and meet market demands.

Employee Performance and Understanding are Group Affairs: Humans make images and impressions of their environment in order to determine appropriate courses of actions. As they seek to find ways of achieving their goals they often look to the norms and values of their social networks to reinforce these beliefs. These social networks provide the employee with the methodology and their perceived value and place within society. Poor social networks will result in increasingly poor choices while strong positive networks will lead to stronger choices. Organizations can encourage stronger decisions by developing norms, practices, and social outlets that encourage higher levels of thinking and development.

Expanding Institutional Orders: Organizations are groups of people who eventually integrate into a bounded rationality. This rationality impacts workers throughout their lives in a world where career and employment opportunities shift on a regular basis. The logic of employment and needs attainment learned through such bounded rationality creates an expanding institutional order as workers integrate such concepts into their lives and carry them to the next workplace thereby perpetuating the order further. The knowledge coming from successful employees and employers is copied and emulated creating new business models that develop and innovate off each other.

Technology as a Medium to Expansion: Information is moving at lightning speed. Technology is the medium by which this information passes from person to person and organization to organization. New developments and technological advancements require an innovative employee that is able to think of new solutions to fulfill customer needs in a high tech environment. As these new products and services solve problems within the marketplace, the advancement spreads quickly among firms who utilize this technology in developing creative capital for American businesses and more revenue for their government.

Employee Performance as a Matter of Habit: Employees enter the workplace with perceptions of how an organization operates in terms of job requirements and reward attainment. They first attempt to use existing patterns within the workplace to successfully navigate the environment and then seek new patterns when existing ones are not rewarded. Through feedback and environmental cues such employees begin to adjust their patterns to a more productive end. Policies and procedures are designed to ensure that employees follow particular work patterns that are most beneficial for the organization. Improving organizational structure, relationships, and expectations can adjust the patterns employees use to a higher level of profits and personal development.

Economic Hubs and Economic Vines: The world contains economic hubs where successful culture has met with appropriate organizational development to create areas of mutual influence. The organizations within these hubs encourage greater rates of growth and then sell the outputs of that production on the international market. The influence of the economic hub fosters the financial well-being of local citizens. Knowledge and financial influence propels outward to other areas and economic arenas as it looks for resources to further its patterns of growth. Economic hubs attract people with the skills and mindset to success within this atmosphere that perpetuates the system.

Management Responsibility: Management is not just the administrators of the physical aspects of labor but also the caretakers of intellectual capital. Strong management encourages employees to think for themselves, come up with solutions, and apply them to the organization. Through trust of expectation, performance and reward employees will create greater levels of economic output. The stronger the skill of managers to influence larger groups and capitalize on their resources for personal and organizational advancement the more worth the manager has to the organization and society.

Values and Norms Create Methods of Logical Thinking:
Values and norms within society create methods of thinking that project toward certain patterns of organizational and societal growth. How an employee uses logic, connects information, and capitalizes on that information is embedded within the organizational and societal culture. Developing strong organizational cultures also develops national cultures through pressure for change as successful groups become emulated. Employees will eventually abandon values and norms that are

spoken but have little practical utility in the environment when those choices are no longer reinforced through the environment.

Systems and Structures Create Reality: Economic systems, financial chains, social networks, education, and organizational structures create an understanding of the environment that constitutes an employee's understanding of reality. When such systems are not in alignment with national needs they detract organizational resources, employee effort, and the value of products away from societal enhancement. Financial resources and organizational structure should be based on key values or mission statements that are in alignment with societal needs in order to develop employee understanding of productive behavior and their opportunities for contribution. Over time it is these environmental cues that develop underlying logic and value systems.

Societal Development is on a Trajectory Upward: Society continues to develop and expand upward into higher states of existence. When society is faced with a challenge and can meet that challenge it moves upward. If it fails to muster its resources to overcome those challenges it will begin a process of disintegration. The Roman Empire collapsed when its leadership and population no longer mustered the ability to maintain the focus of smaller societies connected to Rome's logistical networks (i.e. the road). Rome's failures were the failures of its leaders to adapt their thinking and the emulation of that failure among its people. Confusion of purpose and loss of upward momentum results from the inability of its people to understand and adapt to new market realities. Those cultures that do not bend will eventually be broken by those that have developed conclusions that are more beneficial and effective.

Socialized Values Influence Organizational and National Success: Each generation socializes the next generation to those values which are viewed as productive and socially appropriate. These basic values created a root whereby all other thinking and understanding expands outward creating more complexity with time and maturity. The very quality of a nation's labor force is based on those socialized values and the education employees gain to influence their environments. Productive values mixed with education creates the most effective employees due to their ability to think of solutions and influence the environment in positive ways for individual, organizational and societal growth.

Critical Thinking and Environmental Success: Critical thinking allows individuals to see themselves and their world in a more accurate light. Fostering critical thinking offers employees a chance to make better meaning of the information available to them, categorize it properly, and choose courses of actions that are most appropriate for the strategic outcomes of both themselves and their workplace. Managers and organizations that rely on heavily on power and coercion will find that employees will no longer bring forward great ideas forcing the intellectual capital to decline to the detriment of the organization and the workers therein employed. Organizations that retain critical thinkers will have an easier time overcoming market challenges due to their ability to produce focused results and having anchors for new thinking when it is called upon.

History, Philosophy/Religion, and Science: History, philosophy/religion, and science filters all contribute to the ability to perceive the world, self and society in a progressive light. Developing human capital that can see their world and their shared responsibilities accurately will help them commit more closely to their work functions and the organizations that offer them the chance to fulfill these obligations. History, Philosophy/Religion and Science give guidance to employees who desire to increase their skill and contribute effectively to individual, organization, and national resource obtainment.

Cultural Identity and Conflict: Cultural identity is a perception based upon the way someone has been socialized to understand and navigate the world. In the global age new cultural identities develop that are more enlightened and accepting of differences. It provides for a stronger potential of understanding of various cultures and how to work in and with those cultures. Failure to understand others limits the productive capacity of the organization, the decisions being enacted, and the marketability of the products. It creates higher levels of conflict that waste resources and squanders future opportunities. On a national scale, it can damage international relationships and the ability to engage others in ways that are productive and healthy.

The Mind as an Unexplored Avenue of Growth: The mind is the next generation of market development. Technology is the extension of the mental abilities of people to create higher levels of environmental influence. It is the ability of this mind to synthesis masses of information, develop new pathways for growth, and project those understandings into the environment. It is through this mental, emotional, physical and virtual interaction that the mind adapts to its environment and creates more powerful resonations of business opportunities and environmental adjustments.

Engagement, Fear and Trust: Employees naturally fear change as the potential outcomes are unknown. This fear can create in action. They will also be required to expend energy in order to successfully master the new skills needed to overcome those challenges. Managers who can offer appropriate information, share their vision, support employee development, and maintain relationships through engagement will increase trust and reduce fear. It is this trust that encourages employees to accept change instead of using resources to block change in order to avoid the dissonance associated with such feelings.

Orders of the Mind: Complexity of thought and orders of conscious awareness are something that develops over a person's lifetime. The stronger the mental schematic the more details and associated constructs that can be used to solve life problems. Developing and exposing employees to increasing information requires higher associated levels of thinking. Through such higher order thinking employees can weigh the multiple possibilities and make meaning from large arenas of data. Mental development is part biological by nature but it is the environment that provides the greatest opportunities for intellectual enhancement.

The Disadvantaged Global Generation: The global generation is coming into the labor market at a time where high education is needed and international competition is fierce. The development of a looming crisis has been decades in the making and will impact the viability of economic systems as well as methodologies of life. A single misplaced generation can change the course of a nation. What was sow years ago is now being reaped today. Engagement and opportunity will be important to ensure this generation develops at an optimal level.

The American Advantage: Americans have the ability to adjust their behavior based upon new market realities. It is not a perfect alignment nor is it an easy one but through the concepts of life, liberty and the pursuit of happiness the essential elements for a strong capitalistic system that affords enhanced levels of personal and societal development can be found. The concepts of employee satisfaction, motivation, and innovation help to give modern practical utility to root cultural concepts by focusing on practical business imperatives. **I Still Believe!**

References

Abelson, R. (1985). A variance explained paradox: when a little is a lot. *Psychological Bulletin, 97.*

Adair, J. (2006). *Leadership and motivation.The fifty-fifty rule and the eight key principles of motivating others.*Kogan Page, London and Philadelphia.

Akerlof, G &Kranton, R (2010).*Identity Economics: how our identities shape our work, wages, and well-being.* Princeton University Press.

Albanese, R. (1970). Overcoming resistance to stability: a time to move; a time to pause. *Business Horizons, 13* (2).

Alexander, S. & Ruderman, M. (1987).The role of procedural and distributive justice in organizational behavior. Social Justice Research, 1.

Altman, B. (2009). Determining US workers' training: history and constructivist paradigm. *Journal of european Industrial Training, 33* (6), 490-491.

Amabile, T., Barsade, S., Mueller, J.., & Staw, B. (2005).Affect and creativity at work.*Administrative Science Quarterly, 50*: 367–403.

Amit, R. and Schoemaker, P. (1993)Strategic Assets and Organizational Rent. *Strategic Management Journal 14*, 33–46.

Andrews, G. (1994). Mistrust, the hidden obstacle to empowerment.*Human Resource Magazine, 39* (9).

Argyle, M. (1989). Is a nonverbal communication a kind of language? A R*eview of General Semantics, 46* (2).

Aron, E. (2006). The clinical implications of Jung's concept of sensitiveness.*Journal of Jungian Theory and Practice, 8* (3). http://www.junginstitute.org/pdf_files/JungV8N2p11-44.pdf

Aron, E. N. (2004). "Revisiting Jung's Concept of Innate Sensitiveness".*Journal of Analytical Psychology* **49** (3): 337–367.

Austin, J. & Vancouver, J. (1996). Goal constructs in psychology: Structure, process, and content. *Psychological Bulletin, 120,* 338–375.

Avolio, B. & Bass, B. (1995). Individual consideration viewed at multiple levels of analysis: a multi level framework for examining the diffusion of transformational leadership. *Leadership Quarterly, 6* (2).

Ayres, C. (1958). *Veblen's Theory of Instincts Reconsidered.* In Thorstein Veblen: A Critical Reappraisal, edited by D. F. Dowd, 25-37. Ithaca, N.Y.: Cornell University Press, 1958.

Baldoni, J., (2005). *Motivation Secrets.Great Motivation Secrets of Great Leaders.* [Online] Available: http://govleaders.org/motivation_secrets.htm

Balvociute, R. &Bakanauskiene (2011). Research on work incentives and motivating factors in manufacturing and service sector companies of SiauliaCity.*Social Research, 4* (25).

Barnard, C. (1938). *The functions of the Executive.* Cambridge, MA: Harvard University Press.

Barsalou, L. (2008). Grounded Cognition. *Annual Review of Psychology, 59,* 617–45

Bartlett, T. (August 17, 2012). Dusting off God: A new science of religion says belief has gotten a bad rap. *The Chronicle Review, LVIII* (44).

Beauboeuf, T. (2008).Mammy me?'Strong' Black women at work.Conference Papers--American Sociological Association, 2008 Annual Meeting, 1, 17.

Beck, A. (1999). *Prisoners of Hate: The Cognitive Basis of Anger, Hostility, and Violence.* New York, NY: HarperCollins Publishers Inc.

Bens, D., Goodman, T. &Neamtiu, M. (2012). Does investment-related pressure lead to misreporting? An analysis of reporting following M&A transactions. *Accounting Review, 87* (3).

Behrmann M, Geng JJ, Shomstein S. Parietal cortex and attention. Current Opinion in Neurobiology. 2004;14:212–17.

Berger, P. &Luckman, T. (1966). *The social construction of reality: a treatise in the sociology of knowledge.* Anchor Books, Garden City, N.Y.

Berkowitz, C. (1972). Social norms, feeling and other factors affecting helping behavior and altruism.In (Berkowitz (ED), *Advances in Experimental Social Psychology* (6, pp 63-108). New York: Academic Press.

Bernthal, W. (1978).Matching German culture and management style: A book review essay.*Academy of Management Review, 3* (1).

Biddle, B. & Thomas, E. (1966). *Role theory: Concepts and research.* New York: John Wiley & Sons.

Bink, M. L., & Marsh, R. L. (2001).Cognitive regularities in creative activity.*Review of General Psychology, 4,* 59-78.

Blanchard, N. & Thacker, J. (2010).*Effective Training: Systems, strategies and practices (fourth edition).*Pentice Hall, N.J.

Boens, E. (2006). Positive communication: non-profit used innovative tools to motivate employees & improve bottom line. *Industrial Safety & Hygiene News, 40* (6).

Boyer, E. (1990). *Scholarship reconsidered: priorities for the professoriate.* Carnegie Foundation: Princeton, N.J.

Bragues, G. (2006). Seek the good life, not money: The Aristotelian approach to business ethics. *Journal of Business Ethics, 67* (4).

Brette, O. (2003) Thorstein Veblen's Theory of Institutional Change: Beyond Technological Determinism. *European Journal of the History of Economic Thought 10,* (3), 455-477.

Bronowski, J. &Mazlish, B. (1960). *The Western Intellectual Tradition.* Harper Perennial, NY.

Bruggemann, A. (1974). ZureUntersheildingverschiedenerformenvon'arbeitszufried enheit (Differentiation of various forms of job satisfaction), Arbeit und Leistung, 11, 283-284.

Bruner, J. (1986). *Actual minds, possible worlds.* Cambridge, MA: Harvard University Press.

Burgess, R. (1929), 'Urban Areas', in T. Smith and L. White, eds., Chicago: An Experiment in Social Science, 113–38. Chicago: University of Chicago Press.

Bush, G. (1990). "I'd prefer not to": A research note on resistance to office work in some post World War II American films. *Labor History, 31* (3).

Camilovic, S. & Vidojevic, V. (2007).*Basics of human resource management.* Belgrade; Tekon.

Capus, S. (August 25th, 2012). Capus: Who gets your education vote? *Detroit Free Press.* Retrieved August 25th, 2012 from http://www.detroitnews.com/article/20120925/OPINION01 /209250319/1008/opinion01/Capus-Who-gets-your-education-vote-

Chomsky, N. (1966) *Topics in the Theory of Generative Grammar.* The Hague: Mouton.

Chui, A. Lloyd, A. & Kwok, C. (2002). The determination of capital structure: is national culture a missing piece of the puzzle? *Journal of International Business Studies, 33* (1).

Chesbrough, H. (2003). *Open innovation: The new imperative for creating and profiting from technology.* Boston: Harvard Business School Press.

Cuddy-Kene, M. (2012). Narration, navigation, and non-conscious thought: neuroscientific and literary approaches to the thinking body. *University of Toronto Quarterly, 79* (2).

Cohen, W. M., &Levinthal, D. A. (1990). Absorptive capacity: A new perspective on learning and innovation. *Administrative Science Quarterly, 35*(1), 128–152.

Colander, D. (2011).The economics profession, the financial crisis, and method. *Journal of Economic Methodology, 17* (4).

Collins, R. (1998). *The Sociology of Philosophies: A Global Theory of Intellectual Change. Cambridge,* MA: Harvard University Press.

Contiu, L. (2011). The influence of culture on organizational structures in Romania. *Studiauniversitatis Petru Major-Philogia,* 10.

Copland, S. (2008). Reading in the blend: collaborative conceptual blending in the silent traveler narratives, 16 (2).

"Declining Employee". (2002). Declining employee trust poses threat. *Financial Executive, 18* (7).

Csikszentmihalyi, M. (1996).*Creativity, flow and the psychology of discovery and invention.*New York, NY: HarperCollins.

Damasio, A. (1994*). Descartes' Error: Emotion, Reason and the Human Brain.* New York: G.P. Putnam's Sons

Davidson, D. (1975). Thought and talk in S. Guttenplan (ed.), *Mind and Language* (Clarendon Press, Oxford, 1975), p. 20.

Davis, K. (1962). Human relations at work. New York: McGraw Hill.

De Dreu, C., Weingart, L., & Kwon, S. (2000). Influence of social motives on integrative negotiation: A meta-analytic review and test of two theories. *Journal of Personality and Social Psychology, 78*: 889–905.

De Dreu, C., et. al. (2011). Group creativity and innovation: a motivated information processing perspective. *Psychology of Aesthetics, Creativity and the Arts, 5* (1).

D'Monte, L. (January 21, 2013).World jobless number seen rising to record high in 2013: ILO.The Wall Street Journal. Retrieved January 21, 2013 from http://www.livemint.com/Politics/FRKd5Zd2Hdk04fYvT3 AoQN/World-jobless-number-seen-rising-to-record-high-in-2013-ILO.html

Dobrescu, M. & Paicu, C. (2012). New approaches to business cycle theory in current economic science. *Theoretical & Applied Economics, 19* (7).

Douglas, K. (2007). Subconscious: the other you. *New Scientist, 196* (2632).

Drucker.Claremont Graduate University. Retrieved July 8th, 2012 from https://docs.google.com/document/d/1-xzXHBfwv-c_b0D4ReA3HErvXvXWREM8rJBlcQkOj28/edit?pli=1

Dumbrava, G. & Koronka, A. (2009). "Actions speak louder than words"-Body language in business communication. *Annals of the University of Petronsani Economics, 9 (*3).

Durkheim, Emile. *The Division of Labor in Society.* Trans. Lewis A. Coser. New York: Free Press, 1997, pp. 39, 60, 108.

Dutton, K. (Oct. 26th, 2012). Psychopathy's double edge. The Chronicle Review, LIX, (9).

Edelman, G. & Tononi, G. (2000).*A Universe of Consciousness: How Matter becomes Imagination.* NY: Basic Books. ISBN: 978-0-465-01377-7

Edgell, S. (1975).Thorstein Veblen's Theory of Evolutionary Change.*American Journal of Economics and Sociology 34*, (3), 267-280.

Ehrlich, C. (2006). The EFQM-Model and work motivation. Total Quality Management, 17 (2).

Eisenbeiss, K., Otten, S. (2008). When do employee identify? An analysis of cross-sectional and longitudinal predictors of training group and organizational identification.*Journal of Applied Social Psychology, 38* (8).

Foucault, M. (1973). *Madness and civilization.Translated by Richard Howard.* New York: Random House.

Fenton-O'Creeyv, M. (1998). Employee involvement and the middle manager: evidence from a survey of organizations. *Journal of Organizational Behavior, 19* (1).

Ferster, C. (1967). Arbitrary and natural reinforcement.The Psychological Record, 17 (3).

Fischman, J. (2012, September 28th). *The marketplace in your brain.*The Chronicle Review.

Ford, R. & Fottler, M. (1995). Empowerment: a matter of degree. *Academy of Management Executive, 9.*

Fontevechia, A. (2012). China to unleash one trillion RMB Fiscal Stimulus, Nomura Says. Forbes. Retreived September 10th, 2012 from http://www.forbes.com/sites/afontevecchia/2012/09/10/chin as-doing-it-beijing-to-unleash-one-trillion-rmb-fiscal-stimulus/

Forsythe, M. (February 8th, 2013). China Passes U.S. to Become World's Biggest Trading Nation. Bloomberg News. Retrieved February 9th, 2013 from http://www.bloomberg.com/news/2013-02-09/china-passes-u-s-to-become-the-world-s-biggest-trading-nation.html

Freedman, J. & Coombs, G. (1996) *Narrative therapy: The social construction of preferred realities.* New York: Norton.

Friedman, M. (2002).*Capitalism and Freedom.* The University of Chicago Press: Chicago, UK.

Friedman, Milton. "The Social Responsibility of Business Is to Increase Its Profits." *New York Times Magazine,* 13 September 1970.

Galin, D. (2004) Aesthetic Experience: Marcel Proust and the Neo-Jamesian Structure of Awareness. *Consciousness and Cognition, 1,* 241-53

Gagne´, M., & Deci, E. (2005). Self-determination theory and work motivation. *Journal of Organizational Behavior, 26*: 331–362.

Garrett, T., and Sobel, R. (2003) The Political Economy of FEMA Disaster Payments. *Economic Inquiry 41* (3): 496–509.

Gaouette, N. (December 10th, 2012). *U.S. Intelligence Agencies See a Different World in 2030.*Bloomberg. Retrieved December 10th, 2012 from http://www.bloomberg.com/news/2012-12-10/u-s-intelligence-agencies-see-a-different-world-in-2030.html

George, J. (2007). Creativity in organizations.In J. P. Walsh & A. P. Brief (Eds.), *Academy of Management annals, vol. 1*: 439–477.

Gergen, K. (1985). The social constructionist movement in modern psychology. *American Psychologist*, 40, 266-275

Gerchikov, V. (2005).Tipologicheskaiaknotseptsiiatrudovoimotivatsii.Cha st'1.Motivatsiia I oplatatruda no. 2

Gerchirove, V. (2008).Upravleniepersonalom: rabotnik-samyieffektivnyiresurskompanni: ucheb. Posob.Moscom: infram.

Giddens, A. (1990), The Consequences of Modernity. Cambridge: Polity.

Gilley, A., Thompson, J., & Gilley, J.. (2012). Leaders and Change: Attend to the Uniqueness of Individuals. *Journal of Applied Management and Entrepreneurship, 17*(1),

Giles, C. (January 15th, 2013). World Bank cautions on economic stimulus. Financial Times. Retrieved January 15th, 2013 from http://www.ft.com/intl/cms/s/0/405d5110-5f31-11e2-8250-00144feab49a.html#axzz2I6freHve

Gittell, J. & Von Nordenflycht, A. &Kochan, T. (2004). Mutual gains or zero sum? Labor relations and firm performance in the airline industry.*Industrial& Labor Relations Review, 57* (2).

Glimcher, P. (2004). Decisions, uncertainty, and the brain: the science of neuroeconomics. MIT Press: UK.

Goffman, E. (1963). Stigma.Prentice-Hall, Englewood Cliffs, N. J.

Gorden, W., Infante, D., and Graham, E. (1988).Corporate conditions conducive to employee voice.A subordinate perspective.*Employee Responsibilities and Rights Journal, 1* (2), 101-111

Gorden, et. al. (1992). Employee perceptions of corporate partnership: an affective-moral quid pro quo. *Employee Responsibilities and Rights Journal, 5* (1).

Goodman, D & Schneider, R. (September 3rd, 2012). Snyder sets brisk pace in Mackinac Bridge Walk. ABC Chanel 13. Retrieved September 3rd, 2012 from http://www.13abc.com/story/19445116/snyder-sets-brisk-pace-in-mackinac-bridge-walk

Goody, J. (1961). Religion and ritual: the definitional problem. *British Journal of Sociology, 12*, p 156.

"GOP Delegates" (August 21st, 2012). GOP delegates want tough talk at convention. Northwestern Ohio. Retrieved August 21st, 2012 from http://www.northwestohio.com/news/story.aspx?id=790911

Graham, J. (1989*). Organizational citizenship behavior: Construct redefinition, operationalization, and validation.*Unpublishedpaper.Department of Management, Loyola University, Chicago.

Grant, A. & Berry, J. (2011). The necessity of others is the mother of invention: intrinsic and pro-social motivations, perspective taking, and creativity. *Academy of Management Journal, 54* (1).

Greeley, B. (August 6th, 2012). Bernanke to Economists.More Philosophy Please. Bloomberg Businessweek. Retrieved August 6th, 2012 from http://www.businessweek.com/articles/2012-08-06/bernanke-to-economists-more-philosphy-please

Greenberg, J. (1990). Organizational justice: yesterday, today and tomorrow. *Journal of Management, 16.*

Greenspan, A. (2008). *The Age of Turbulence: Adventures in a New World.* Penguin Group: NY.

Griesinger, D. (1990). The human side of economic organization.*Academy of Management Review, 15* , 478-499.

Guthrie, J. (July 18th, 2012). Unmasked banks face tough questions. Financial Times. Retrieved July 19th, 2012 from ft.com

Hackman, J. & Lawler, E. (1971). Effects of job redesign: a field experiment.*Journal of Applied Social Psychology, 3* (1)

Hackman, J. & Oldham, R. (1976). Motivation through the design of work: test of a theory. *Organizational Behavior and Human Performance, 16*, pp. 250-279.

Halliday, M. (1993).Toward a Language-Based Theory of Learning. *Linquistings and Education, 5*, 93-116

Heavey, S. &Lawder, D. (October 25th, 2012). In rare show of unity, U.S. ceo's call for deficit fix. Chicago Tribune.

Retrieved October 25th, 2012 from
http://www.chicagotribune.com/business/sns-rt-us-congress-deficitbre89o09u-20121024,0,7872398.story

Heckhausen, H. &Rehinburg, F. (1980). Learning motivation in education, newly considered. *Unterrichtswissenschaft, 1.* pp 7-47.

Heilbroner, R. (1999). The worldly philosophers (seventh edition). Simon & Schuster, NY.

Heimer, C. and Staffen, L. (1998). *For the Sake of the Children: The Social Organization of Responsibility in the Hospital and the Home.* Chicago: University of Chicago Press.

Helms, M. (August 7th, 2012). Detroit's lemonaid kid, 9, presents check to city. Detroit Free Press. Retrieved August 7th, 2012 from http://www.freep.com/article/20120807/NEWS01/1208070 39/Boy-9-who-raised-cash-for-Detroit-with-lemonade-stand-presents-check-to-city

Hennessey, B. ,& Amabile, T. (2010). Creativity.*Annual Review of Psychology, 61,* 569–598.

Heylighen, F. (2003). Characteristics and problems of the gifted: neural propagation depth and flow motivation as a model of intelligence and creativity. Cognition, 1-47

Henderson, S. (August 8th, 2012). Intolerable Waste in Detroit's Water Department.DetroitFreePress. Retrieved August 9th, 2012 from http://www.freep.com/article/20120809/COL33/308090096 /Stephen-Henderson-Intolerable-waste-in-Detroit-s-Water-Department

Hermann M. (1952) Space and Time" in Hendrik A. Lorentz.Albert Einstein, Hermann Minkowski, and Hermann Weyl. The Principle of Relativity: A Collection of Original Memoirs on the Special and General Theory of Relativity (Dover, New York, 1952).

Hodgson, B. (2001). *Economics as moral science*. New York: Springer.

Hofstede, G. (1991). *Culture and organizations: Software of the mind*. London, UK: McGraw Hill.

Hofstede, G. (1980). *Culture's consequences: International differences in work related values*. Newbury Park, CA: Sage.

Holdsworth, G. (2011). *Economics and the limits of optimization: steps towards extending Bernard Hodgson's Moral Science*.Journal of Business Ethics, 108 (1).

Hollis, M. &Lukes, S. (1982). *Rationality and Relativism.*Basil Blackwell Publisher Limited; UK.

Hollis, M. (1968). Reason and Ritual. *Philosophy, 43*, pp 231-247 doi:10.1017/S0031819100009207

Hornbein, T. (1968).*Everest: The West Ridge*. San Francisco: Sierra Club.

Hotz, R. (June 19th, 2009). A wondering mind heads straight for insight. The Wall Street Journal.Retreived September 2nd, 2012 from http://online.wsj.com/article/SB124535297048828601.html

Hultman, K. (1995). Scaling the Wall of Resistance. *Training & Development, 49* (10).

Huseman, R. & Hatfield, J. (1989).*Managing the equity factor.*Boston Houghton Mifflin.

International Labor Organization (May 8th, 2013). Global employment trends for 2013: a generation at risk. Retrieved May 9th, 2013 from http://www.ilo.org/global/research/global-reports/global-employment-trends/youth/2013/WCMS_212423/lang--en/index.htm

Jacobides., M. G. (2007). The inherent limits of organizational structure and the unfulfilled role of hierarchy: Lessons from a near-war. *Organization Science, 18,* (3), 455-477.

Jacobs, K. &Manzi, T. (February, 2000). Performance indicators and social constructivism: conflict and control in housing management. *Critical Social Policy, 20* (1), 85-103

James, W. (1890) The principles of psychology. Troy, Mo.: Holt, Rinehart & Winston, 2, pg. 550

Jensen, H.(1987). The Theory of Human Nature.*Journal of Economic Issues 21*, (3), 1039-1073.

Jevons, W. (1924). The theory of political economy.*London Journal, 57* (2).

Jones, D. (2012). Servant leadership impact on profit, employee satisfaction, and empowerment within the framework of participative culture in business.*Business Studies Journal, 4* (1).

Jones, G. R. (2007). *Introduction to business: How companies create value for people.* New York: McGraw Hill/Irwin.

Jung, C. Jung. *Psychological Types.*Bollingen Series XX, Volume 6, Princeton University Press, 1971.

Jung, C. (1928) Relations between the ego and the unconscious.CW 7.

C. G. Jung, *The Archetypes and the Collective Unconscious* (London 1996) p. 43

Dimberg, U.; Thunberg, M (2000)."Unconscious facial reactions to emotional facial expressions". *Psychological Science 11 (*1): 86.

Kable, J. and Glimcher, P. (2007).The Neural Correlates of Subjective Value during Intertemporal Choice.*Nature Neuroscience, 10* (12): 1625–33.

Lee, G. (2012). The Keynesian Path to Fiscal Irresponsibility.*Kato Journal, 32* (3).

Katz, D. (1964). The motivational basis of organizational behavior.*Behavioral Science, 9*, 131-146

Kaufmann, W. (1956).Nietsche. Holt, Rinehart and Winston; NY

Kamalian, A., Yaghoubi, N., &Moloudi, J., (2010). Survey of Relationship between Organizational Justice and Empowerment (A Case Study).*European Journal of Economics, Finance and Administrative Sciences, 24*, 165-171.

Kane, K & Montgomery, K. (1998).A framework for understanding disempowerment within organizations.*Human Resource Management, 37* (3/4).

Kappelman, L. &Prybutok, V. (1995). Empowerment, motivation, training, and TQM program implementation success. *Industrial Management, 37*, (3).

Kegan, R. (1984) Prologue: *Construction and Development.* Evolving Self, Cambridge: Harvard University Press

Kelly, G. (1969). *The psychology of personal constructs* (2 vols.) New York: WW Norton.

Kenneth Allan; Kenneth D. Allan (2 November
   2005). *Explorations in Classical Sociological Theory:
   Seeing the Social World.* Pine Forge Press. p. 108. ISBN 1-
   4129-0572-9.

Ketay, S., Hedden, T., Aron, A., Aron, E., Markus, H., &Gabrieli,
   G. (2007). The personality/
   temperament trait of high sensitivity: fMRI evidence for
   independence of cultural context in attentional processing.
   Presented at the Society for Personality and Social
   Psychology, Memphis.

Ketokivi, M. &Castaner, X. (2004).Strategic planning as an
   integrative device. *Administrative Science Quarterly,
   49* (3).

Keynes, J. (1968). *Essays in Persuasion.* W.W. Norton &
   Company, NY

Keynes, J. M. (1936) *The General Theory of Employment, Interest
   and Money.* New York: Harcourt, Brace and Co.

Kunda, Z. (1990). The case for motivated reasoning.*Psychological
   Bulletin, 108*: 480–498.

Kvedaravicius, J. (2005). Organizaciju vystymosi vadyba.*Kaunas:*
   VDU leidykla.

Kindy, K., Fallis, D. &Higham, S. (October 8th, 2012). Congress
   members back legislation that could benefit themselves,
   relatives. The Washington Post. Retrieved October 10th,
   2012 from
   http://www.washingtonpost.com/politics/congress-
   members-back-legislation-that-could-benefit-themselves-
   relatives/2012/10/07/c2fa7d94-f3a9-11e1-a612-
   3cfc842a6d89_story.html

Kinicki, A. &Kreitner, R. (2009). *Organizational Behavior: key concepts, skills & best practices.*Fourth Edition. USA, McGraw-Hill.

King, R. & Bu, N. (2005). Perceptions of the mutual obligations between employees and employers: a comparative study of new generation IT professionals in China and the United States. *International Journal of Human Resource Management, 16* (1).

Krisher, T. (August 9th, 2012). GM CEO says old culture still hinders change. BlueRidgeNow. Retrieved August 15th, 2012 from http://www.blueridgenow.com/article/20120809/APF/1208090816

Kuhn, T. (1996).The structure of scientific revolutions. The University of Chicago Press, IL.

Kurtenbach, E. (September 8th, 2012). China will boost demand to help global recovery. USA Today. Retrieved September 8th, 2012 from http://www.usatoday.com/money/business/story/2012/09/8/china-will-boost-demand-to-help-global-recovery/57697902/1

LaCapra, L. (July 10th, 2012). Many Wall Street Executives Says Wrongdoing is Necessary: Survey. Rueters. Retrieved July 10th, 2012 from http://www.reuters.com/article/2012/07/10/us-wallstreet-survey-idUSBRE86906G20120710

Lacayo, R., Estulin, C. & Jakes, S. (2004). Going up...and up: when height is all that matters. Time, 164/165 (26/1).

Lall, S. (2000) Technological change and industrialization in the Asian newly industrializing economies, in: L. Kim & R. Nelson (Eds) Technology, Learning, and Innovation (Cambridge: Cambridge University Press).

Lambooij, M., et. al. (2007). Encouraging employees to co-operate: the effects of sponsored training and promotion practices on employees' willingness to work overtime. *International Journal of Human Resource Management, 18* (10)

Latham, G. P., & Locke, E.A. (1979), Goal-setting: A motivational technique that works. *Organizational Dynamics, 8* (2): 68-80.

Lawler III, E. & Hackman, R. (1971). Corporate profits and employee satisfaction: must they be in conflict? *California Management Review, 14* (1)

Lawler, E. (1993). From job-based to competency-based organizations.*CEO Publication G*, 93-8 (228)

Lawler, E., Mohrman, S. & Ledford, G. (1992). *Employee involvement and total quality management: practices and results in fortune 1000 companies.* San Francisco: Jossey-Bass.

Leonardi, P. & Barley, S. (June 2010). What's under construction here? Social action, materiality, and power constructivists studies of technology and organizing. *The Academy of Management Annals, 4* (1).

Lickert, R. (1959b). A motivational approach to a modified theory of organizational management. In Haire, M. (ed.). Modern organizational theory: a symposium of foundation for research on human behavior. New York-Wiley, 184-217.

Line, D. & Tyler, T. (1988).*The social psychology of procedural justice.* New York: Plenum Press.

Linn, A. (October 22nd, 2012). Gen X now worries most about retirement. CNBC. Retrieved October 22nd, 2012 from http://www.cnbc.com/id/49505546

Li, J. & Harrison, R. (2008). National culture and the composition and leadership structure of boards of directors. Corporate Governance: *An International Review, 16* (5).

Liu, D., Liao, H. & Loi, R. (2012). The dark side of leadership: a three-level of investigation of cascading effective of abusive supervision on employee creativity. *Academy of Management Journal, 55* (5).

Lewis, K. (2006). Employee perspectives on implementation communication as predictors of perceptions of success and resistance. *Western Journal of Communication, 70* (1).

Lorenzo Ravagli, *Zanders Erzählungen*, Berliner Wissenschafts-Verlag, ISBN 978383051613, pp. 680f

Lucas, R. (1972). Expectations and the Neutrality of Money. *Journal of Economic Theory, 4*, pp. 103-124.

McAdams, D., & de St. Aubin, E. (1992).A theory of generativity and its assessment through self-report, behavioral acts, and narrative themes in autobiography.*Journal of Personality and Social Psychology, 62*: 1003–1015.

Madrick,J. (October, 2012). The anti-economist, the austerity myth. Harper's Magazine, 325 (1949)

Manzoor, Q. (2011). Impact of employees motivation on organizational effectiveness. *Business and Management Strategy, 3* (1).

Martin, J. &Siehl, C. (1971). Organizational culture and counter culture: an uneasy symbiosis. *Organizational Dynamics, 12*, 52-64.

Mas-Colell, M., Whinston, M. & Green.*Microeconomic Theory.* Oxford University Press; Oxford

Matthew, J., Grawhich, & Barber, L., (2009). Are you Focusing both Employees and Organizational Outcomes. *Organizational Health Initiative at Saint Louis University* (ohi.slu@edu), 1-5.

Maylett, T. & Nielsen, J. (Apr 2012). There is no cookie-cutter approach to engagement. *T&D, 66* (4).

McCrae, R.and Costa, P. (1987). Validation of the five-factor model of personality across instruments and observers. Journal of Personality and Social Psychology 52 (1): 81–90.

McHugh, D. (January 21, 2013). Public trust in government, business leaders falls. Detroit Free Press.http://www.freep.com/article/20130121/BUSINESS0 7/130121018/Public-trust-in-government-business-leaders-falls?odyssey=nav|head

McHugh, D. (January 26th, 2013). Davos summit concludes with warnings on global economy. Deseret News. Retrieved January 26th, 2013 from http://www.deseretnews.com/article/765621161/Davos-summit-concludes-with-warnings-on-global-economy.html

McNeese-Smith, D. (1996). Increasing employee productivity, job satisfaction, and organizational commitment.*Hospital& Health Services Administration, 41* (2).

Mehta, R., & Zhu, R. (2009, February 5). Blue or red?Exploring the effect of color on cognitive task performances.*Science, 323,* 1226–1229.

Merrihue, W. &Katzell, R. (1955).ERI-Yardstick of Employee Relations. Harvard Business Review, 33, 91.

Mill, J. (1848). *Principles of Political Economy with Some of their Applications to Social Philosophy.* Retrieved December 15th, 2012 from http://www.efm.bris.ac.uk/het/mill/prin.htm

Miller, D. & Toulouse, J. (1986). Chief executive personality and corporate strategy and structure in small firms. *Management Science, 32* (11).

Miller, K. &Monge, P. (1986). Participation, satisfaction, and productivity: A meta-analytic review. *Academy of Management Journal, 29*, 727-753.

Miller, D. & Form, W. (1951*).Industrial Sociology*. New York: HarperCollins.

Mumford, et. al. (2006). Errors in creative thought? Cognitive biases in complex processing activity. *Journal of Creative Behavior, 40* (2).

Moorman, R. (1993). The influence of cognitive and affective based job measures on the relationship between satisfaction and organizational citizen behavior. *Human Relations, 46* (6).759-776.

Mohrman, S., Gibson, C., & Mohrman, A. Jr. (2001). Doing research that is useful to practice: A
model and empirical exploration. *Academy of Management Journal, 44:* 357–375.

Mohrman, S., Cohen, S. and MohrmanJr, A. (1995). *Designing Team-Based Organizations: New Forms for Knowledge Work.*(Jossey-Bass, San Francisco).

Montana, S. (2006).*Social Capital in Human Service/Child Welfare Organizations: Implications forWork Motivation, Job Satisfaction, Innovation, and Quality* (Doctoral Dissertation). The University of Texas at Austin.Retrieved January 23, 2013 from ProQuest.

Mushipe, Z. (2011). Employee empowerment and job satisfaction: a study of employees in the food manufacturing sector in Zimbabwe. *Interdisciplinary Journal of Contemporary Research in Business, 3* (8).

Nacinovi, I., Galetic, L. & Cavlek N. (2010). Corporate culture and innovation: Implications for reward systems. *International Journal of Social Sciences, 5* (1).

Neuringer, A. & Jensen, G. (2012).The predictably unpredictable operant.Comparative Cognition & Behavior Reviews, 7 (55).

Noefer, K, Stegmaier, R., Molter, B. & Sonntag, K. (2009). A great many things to do and not a minute to spare: Can feedback from supervisors moderate the relationship between skill variety, time pressure and employees' innovative behavior? Creativity Research Journal, 21 (4).

Oppenheimer, D. (2008). The secret life of fluency. *Trends in Cognitive Sciences, 12,* 237–241

Orpen, (1979). The effects of job enrichment on employee satisfaction, motivation, involvement, and performance: a field experiment. *Human Relations, 32,* pp. 189-217.

O'Reilly, A. (December 5th, 2012). Corruption Perception Index Ranks Venezuela as One of World's Most Crooked Countries. Fox News. Retrieved December 9th, 2012 from http://latino.foxnews.com/latino/news/2012/12/05/corruptio n-perception-index-ranks-venezuela-worlds-most-crooked-countries/#ixzz2EgsUiSCJ

Organ, D. (1977). Organizational Citizenship Behavior: The Good Soldier Syndrome. *Lexington, MA:* Lexington Books.

Ortner, S. (1979), "On Key Symbols," Lensa, W. and Voght. E. Reading in Comparative Religion: An Anthropological Approach, New York: Basic Books.

Ott, E., Grebogi, C. &Yorke, J. (1990).*"Controlling Chaos," physical review letters, 64* (11).

Pagel, M. (2012).Wired for Culture: Origins of the Human Social Mind. NY: W.W. Norton & Company, Inc.

Poyatos, L. (1993). *Paralanguage.A linguistic and interdisciplinary approach to interactive speech and sound.* Amsterdam: John Benjamins.

Nelson, O. (1977). People and Performance: The Best of Peter Drucker on Management. Harper & Row, NY.

Nordgren, J. (2006). Modern age, 1900-2000: a biographical dictionary of western culture.

Nussbaum-Gomes, M. (1994).The subconscious in organizational control. International Journal of Comparative Sociology, 35 (1/2)

Phromket, C., Thanyaphricak, V. &Phromket, C. (2012).An empirical study of organizational justice as a mediator of relationships among organizationa learning culture, employee satisfaction, and employee commitment in Rajamangala University of Technology IsanSaknonNakhon Campus. *Review of Business Research, 12* (2).

Pew Research Center (April 26th, 2012). Growing Gap in Favorable Views of Federal, State Governments. Retrieved January 27th, 2013 from http://www.people-press.org/2012/04/26/growing-gap-in-favorable-views-of-federal-state-governments/
Polanyi, K. (1968). The great transformation: the political and economic origins of our time. Beacon Press. Boston, NY

Porter, L. & Lawler, E. (1968).*Managerial Attitudes and Performance.* Homewood, IL: Richard D. Irwin, Inc.

Potter, G. (1994), Criminal Organisations. Illinois: Waveland Press.

Poling, et. al. (2001). Chapter 2: Principles of Learning : Respondent and Operant Conditioning and Human Behavior. Handbook of Organizational Performance: Behavior Analysis & Management.

"Purdue Research". (2004. Purdue research links employee satisfaction, profits. Purdue University. Retrieved August 22nd, 2012 fromhttp://www.purdue.edu/uns/html4ever/2004/040913.Oakley.sat.html

Radovanovic, V. & Savic, L. (2012).Motivation and job satisfaction.Determinants of competitiveness.MetalurgiaInternationa, XVII (11).

Radovanovic, V. & Savic, L. (2012).Motivation and job satisfaction-determinants of competitiveness.*Metalurgia International, 17* (11)

Raza, M. & Nawaz, M. (2011). Impact of job enrichment on employees' job satisfaction, motivation, and organizational commitment: evidence from the public sector of Pakistan.*European Journal of Social Studies, 23* (2).

Reilly, M., Minnick, C., &Baack, D. (2011).*The five functions of effective management*. San Diego, CA: Bridgepoint Education.

Resnikoff, N. (April 5th, 2013). Fewer Workers are Looking for Work-Why? MSNBC. Retrieved April 7th, 2013 from http://tv.msnbc.com/2013/04/05/fewer-americans-are-working-or-even-looking-for-work-why/

Ridley, M. (2011). The Rational Optimist: How prosperity evolves. UK: Harper-Collins Publishers.

Robinson, L. (2007). Trust your gut. *Business Book Summaries, 1* (1).

Roe, A. (1956).The psychology of occupations. New York: Wiley.

Rosen, H. (1996). *Meaning-Making Narratives: Foundations for constructivist and social constructivist psychotherapy.* San Francisco: Jossey-Bass.

Roskes, M., De Drew, C. & Nijstad, B. (2012) Necessity Is the Mother of Invention: Avoidance Motivation Stimulates Creativity Through Cognitive Effort. *Journal of Personality and Social Psychology, 103* (2)

Rukhmani, K., Ramesh, M., &Jayakrishnan, J., (2010).Effect of Leadership Styles on Organizational Effectiveness.*European Journal of Social Sciences, 15* (3), 365-369.

Ruff, C., Guiseppe, U. and Fehr, E. (2011).Transcranial Direct Current Stimulation of Dorsolateral Prefrontal Cortex Changes Social Norm Compliance.*University of Zurich, Department of Economics.*

Rugaber, C. (August 6th, 2012). Are you happy? Ben Bernanke wants to know. Mercury News. Retrieved August 6th, 2012 from http://www.mercurynews.com/business/ci_21248788/are-you-happy-ben-bernanke-wants-know

Ryan, R. & Deci, E. (2000).Self-determination theory and the facilitation of intrinsic motivation, social development, and well-being.*American Psychologist, 55*: 68–78.

Sakkab, N. Y. (2002). Connect & develop complements: *Research & develop at P&G. Research Technology Management, 45,* 38–45.

Salter, et. al. (2008). Google: the faces and voices of the world's most innovative company. Fast Company, 123, p74-91

Santi, S. (2000).Non-verbal communication.R*outledge Encyclopedia of Language Teaching & Learning.*

Sapir, E. (1929). the status of linguistics as a science. *Language, 5,* p. 209

Savareikiene, D. (2011). *Darbuotoju poreikiu tenkinimu grindziamas darbo motyvacijos proceso vystymasi organizacijoje.Daktaro disertacija.* Kaunas: Vytauto Didziojo universiteto leidykla

Savareikiene, D. (2012). *Motyvo interpretacija motyvacijoje.Ekonomika ir vadyba: aktualijos ir perspektyvos, 1* (25).

Schlick, M. (1936).Meaning and verification.*The Philosophical Review, 46,* pp. 261

Schumpeter, J. (1950) *Capitalism, Socialism, and Democracy* (New York: Harper).

Sideridis, et. al. (2006).Predicting LD on the Basis of Motivation, Metacognition, and Psychopathology: An ROC Analysis.*Journal of Learning Disabilities, 39* (3).

Silvius, G. (2008). The impact of national cultures on business & IT alignment.*Communications of the IIMA,* 8 (2).

Shalley, C. E. (1991). Effects of productivity goals, creativity goals, and personal discretion on individual creativity. Journal of Applied Psychology, 76, 179-185.

Shalley, C., Zhou, J., & Oldham, G. (2004). The effects of personal and contextual characteristics on creativity: Where should we go from here? *Journal of Management, 30*: 933–958.

Sherman, H. & Hunt, E. (2008).*Spread of the business cycle. Economics: An introduction and progressive views* (6th Edition). Armonk, NY: ME. Sharp.

Simpson, I. (April 15th, 2013). Opinion of federal government hits record low: poll. Reuters. Retreived April 15th, 2013 http://www.reuters.com/article/2013/04/15/us-usa-politics-poll-idUSBRE93E0T120130415

Smith, D..(1987). *The Everyday World as Problematic: A Feminist Sociology.* Boston: Northeastern University Press.

Speitzer, G. &Porath, C. (2012).Creating sustainable performance.*Harvard Business Review, 90* (1/2)

Spreitzer, G. (1995). Psychological empowerment in the workplace: dimensions, measurement and validation. *Academy of Management Journal, 38*

Spender, J. (1996) "Organizational knowledge, learning and memory: Three concepts in search of a theory", Journal of Organizational Management, 9, p.63-78

Speitzer, G. &Porath, C. (2012).Creating sustainable performance. Harvard Business Review, 90 (1/2)

Suomi SJ. Uptight and laid-back monkeys: individual differences in the response to social challenges. In: Brauth SE, Hall WS, Dooling RJ, editors. Plasticity of Development. Cambridge, MA: MIT Press; 1991. pp. 27–56

Teece, D. J. (2006).Reflections on "Profiting from innovation."*Research Policy, 35, 1131–1146.*

Temple-West, P. (January 9th, 2013). IRS watchdog urges simpler tax code to cut costs, confusion. Reuters. Retrieved January 9th, 2013 from http://www.reuters.com/article/2013/01/09/usa-tax-taxpayer-advocate-idUSL1E9C7CFW20130109

"The Lost Decade" (2012).The lost decade of the middle class.Pew Research Center. Retrieved August 22nd, 2012 from http://www.pewsocialtrends.org/2012/08/22/the-lost-decade-of-the-middle-class/

"The World's Best" (September 8th, 2012). The world's best (and worst) economies. 24/7 Wall street. Retrieved September 8th, 2012 from http://247wallst.com/2012/09/07/the-worlds-best-and-worst-economies/

The 2012 Long-Term Budget Outlook. (June 5th, 2012). Congressional Budget Office. Retrieved January 14th, 2013 from http://www.cbo.gov/publication/43288

Thomas, K. & Velthouse, B. (1990). Cognitive elements of empowerment: an interpretive model of task motivation. *Academy of Management Review, 15.*

Tobin, D. (1996) *"Transformational Learning – Renewing Your Company Through Knowledge and Skills"* John Wiley & Sons, NY

Tolman, E. (1932) Purposive behavior in animals and man. New York: Century, 1932.

Tser-Yieth, C. Hwang, S. &Liv, Y. (2012). Antecedents of the voluntary performance of employees: clarifying the roles of employee satisfaction and trust. *Public Personnel Management, 41* (3).

Turque, B. (September 9th, 2012). Romney, Ryan defend economic proposals, but provide few specifics. The Washington Post. Retrieved September 9th, 2012 from http://www.washingtonpost.com/politics/2012/09/09/cd7e0582-fa7b-11e1-ab03-6dd8b366b547_story.html

Tyler, M. (August 18th, 2012). President Obama pushes to save education jobs. *Atlanta Blackstar.*Retrieved August 18th,

2012 from http://atlantablackstar.com/2012/08/18/obama-pushes-to-save-education-jobs/

U.S. Census Bureau (2012).U.S. Trade in Goods and Services. Retrieved January 15th, 2013 from http://www.census.gov/foreign-trade/statistics/historical/gands.txt

Van de Vijver, F. (2008). Personality assessment of global talent: conceptual and methodological issues. International Journal of Testing, 8 (4), 304-314

Veblen, T (1898). The Instinct of Workmanship and the Irksomeness of Labor.*American Journal of Sociology 4*, (2), 187-201.

Vladivostok, R. (2012). APEC wraps up with joint commitment on development. English News. Retrieved September 9th, 2012 from http://www.blogger.com/blogger.g?blogID=64001592 02747408925#editor/target=post;postID=38076806327027 03639

von Neumann, J., & Morgenstern, O. (1944). *Theory of games and economic behavior.* Princeton: Princeton University Press.

Vroom, V. (1964). Work and Motivation.Jossey-Bass Publishers; San Francisco

Wen-Chin, L. & Wei-Tao, T. (2006).Organizational justice, motivation to learn, and training outcomes.*Social Behavior & personality: An International Journal, 34* (5).

Westjon, S., Singh, N. & Magnusson, P. (2012). Responsiveness to global and local consumer culture positioning: a personality and collective identity perspective. Journal of International Marketing, 20 (1).

White, R. (1959). Motivation reconsidered: the concept of competence. *Psychol. Rev., 66*, 297-333.

Whorf, B. (1954). Language, thought, and reality (MIT press, Boston, and Wiley, New York).p. 213.

Wiley, C. (1997). What motivates employees according to over 40 years of motivational surveys.International Journal of Manpower, 18 (3).

Wilson, G. (September 4th, 2012). US debt tops $16 trillion: So who do we owe most of that money to? Fox News. Retrieved September 4th, 2012 from http://www.foxnews.com/politics/2012/09/04/who-do-owe-most-that-16-trillion-to-hint-it-isnt-china/#ixzz25ZGjhoFx

Wilson, E. (1999). *Consilience: The Unity of Knowledge.* New York, New York: Vintage.

World Development Report (2013). World Bank. Washington DC.

Worthy, J. (1950).Organizational Structure and employee morale.AmerSociol Rev 15, 169-179.

Wunderlich, K., Rangel, A. & O'Doherty, J. (2010). Economic Choices Can Be Made Using Only Stimulus Values. *PNAS, 107* (34): 15005–10

Yazdani, B., Yaghoubi, N., &Giri, E., (2011). Factors affecting the Empowerment of Employees. *European Journal of Social Sciences, 20* (2), 267-274

Zammuto, R. (1982). *Assessing Organizational Effectiveness.*State University of New York Press, Albany, NY.

Zajonc, R. (1980) Feeling and Thinking: Preferences Need No Inferences. American*Psychologist 35* (2): 151-75.

Zhou, Y., Zhang, Y. & Montoro, S. (2009). How do the reward approaches affect employees' innovation behaviors?--An empirical study in Chinese Enterprises. *Academy of Management Annual Meeting Proceedings, p. 1-6*, 6